Praise for
How Deep Is Your Love?

How Deep Is Your Love? is an amazing reflection of the love that our heavenly father has for each one of us. What a joy to get to know Sharon over the years and see how she is walking out her life's adventure with Paige and not just surviving but thriving in the journey. It's a delight of my heart when I see parents of special needs children learn to love the child and not see the condition as part of the child's identity. I know that this book will bring so much hope and encouragement to parents of special needs children. Thanks, Sharon, for taking the time to write and to allow us to personally enter into your life process and journey.

—Chris Gore
Bethel Church, Redding, CA
Author, *The Perfect Gift, Seeing the Child, Not the Condition*

As I write this endorsement, I find myself searching for the right words to describe the depth of truth and the power of a mother's love . . . and it left me wanting. I am blessed to know this author and her daughter personally—still I found myself discovering new and wonderful aspects of Sharon and Paige's journey. One of faith, hope, and love. Of strength, determination, creativity, and endurance with joy. *How Deep Is Your Love?* tells a poignant tale of a mother and daughter's bond. And so much more. Sharon writes, "I'm believing for Paige to live, and others are believing for her to die." Although this story is wrapped around medical miracles and God encounters, I couldn't help but think of the countless multitudes of people crying out for someone to love them enough to *live*!

This true story will ultimately lead the reader, you and I, to discovering how deep God's love is for each of us. I pray this wonderfully written book finds its way into homes and hearts all across this nation. This is the most beautiful love story I have ever read.

—Mary Jo Pierce
Pastor, author, speaker

How Deep Is Your Love? is a beautiful inspirational story. We believe the words within this book will help thousands of people trust the Lord, the Creator of the universe, with their lives. Since we all face trials in life, Sharon's story of her life journey with Paige reminds us that our loving God is greater than our problems.

We are team leaders with Joni and Friends/Wheels for the World and have watched firsthand how God has opened the door for Sharon to minister His love to moms in Mexico with children with disabilities. As we have observed Paige serving on the mission field, it speaks volumes about Sharon's deep love for Paige, what they have overcome, and where they are today. We are blessed to have Tommy, Sharon, and Paige as a vital part of our team!

—Jim and Kay Christian
Team leaders, Wheels for the World

Sharon shares her poignant story of deep pain but also God's triumphant victory in and through her life. Yet it is not just Sharon's story but also Paige's story of victory. Anyone faced with unexpected, painful life changes can quickly relate to Sharon's story. And if you're not in a similar place, then you know someone who is, and

Sharon's story can give you tools to encourage them. God was not surprised by one detail in Sharon's life, and He was with her each step of the way, giving her and Paige all they needed for each day. He continues to give them what they need and will until His return or they meet Him face to face. I found this to be a heart-grabbing true story that makes you identify with and love Paige and Sharon, but even more the One Who sees them. Like Genesis 16:13, "Then she called the name of the Lord who spoke to her, You are a God who sees," Sharon declares by her words and life, "I too have seen the One Who sees me."

—Donna Wilbanks
Retired BSF teaching leader

It is my honor and pleasure to endorse Sharon's story of her life with Paige. I am Paige's pulmonologist and have been part of Paige's medical team since the beginning. In medicine, we've been taught and trained to be objective when we give counsel to a patient or family about their medical condition and long-term prognosis. I have to admit that Paige has exceeded my expectations. Over the years I have seen Sharon work diligently to maximize Paige's potential. She has worked very hard to take care of Paige's medical needs, allowing her to live a normal life. I have seen the fruit of her dedication and love for Paige. Paige is a kind and polite young lady; she is very happy and enjoys life tremendously. I hope she will continue to thrive and succeed in life. Anyone reading this book will benefit in knowing how deep love can transform a person's life.

—Dr. Sami Hadeed
Pulmonologist

I am Paige Richardson's cardiologist. I have cared for Paige since she was born. Sharon does a remarkable characterization of her premature labor and Paige's birth and the uncovering of multiple problems. The emotional drain on this young mother, coping with the large and overwhelming neonatal intensive care unit, a premature baby with multiple problems, and the ups and downs of her nursery course, is outlined dramatically. Sharon initially reaches out to her family to help deal with Paige's multiple problems and surgeries, as well as dealing with the loss of preconceived perceptions, but then God gives her a different perspective about her daughter, one that changes the course of her life. Although their story is not finished, this book is about loss and triumph, tremendous faith, and Sharon's growth in God. I look forward each year to Paige's heart checkups and to see her smile, and I am always thrilled to see her new accomplishments. This story is special to me since I have a part in it, caring for Paige.

—Dr. Richard Readinger
Cardiologist

HOW DEEP IS YOUR LOVE?

A MOM'S SHATTERED DREAMS ARE **TRANSFORMED INTO SHOWERS OF BLESSINGS**

Sharon Richardson

© 2020 by Sharon Richardson. All rights reserved.

Published by Redemption Press, PO Box 427, Enumclaw, WA 98022.

Toll-Free (844) 2REDEEM (273-3336)

Redemption Press is honored to present this title in partnership with the author. The views expressed or implied in this work are those of the author. Redemption Press provides our imprint seal representing design excellence, creative content, and high quality production.

No part of this publication may be reproduced, stored in a retrieval system, or transmitted in any way by any means—electronic, mechanical, photocopy, recording, or otherwise—without the prior permission of the copyright holder, except as provided by USA copyright law.

Commercial interests: No part of this publication may be reproduced in any form, stored in a retrieval system, or transmitted in any form by any means—electronic, photocopy, recording, or otherwise—without prior permission of the publisher/author, except as provided by the United States of America copyright law.

The Barney and Friends "I Love You" song is used with permission from Lyons Partnership LP.

All Scripture quotations, unless otherwise indicated, are taken from the New King James Version. Copyright © 1982 by Thomas Nelson, Inc. Used by permission. All rights reserved.

Scripture quotations marked NIV are taken from the Holy Bible, New International Version®, NIV® Copyright ©1973, 1978, 1984, 2011 by Biblica, Inc.® Used by permission. All rights reserved worldwide.

Front cover photo by Courtney Raz / JolanJade Photography

Back-cover author photo by Mike Daniel

ISBN 13: 978-1-7347790-1-1 (Paperback)
ISBN 13: 978-1-7347790-0-4 (Spanish Paperback)
ISBN 13: 978-1-68314-957-6 (ePub)
ISBN 13: 978-1-68314-958-3 (Mobi)

Library of Congress Catalog Card Number: 2019918612

Dedication

I DEDICATE THIS BOOK TO my daughter, Paige. Without you, this book never would have been written. Nor would I be the person who I am today. You have opened my eyes to a new world, a new way of living life, one full of great joy and abundant blessings. Because of you, my heart has expanded to greater depths of love. Because of you, I know a God who can do the miraculous.

I love you, Paige, from the deepest part of my heart. Words will never be able to express the fullness of my love for you. You are beautiful to me inside and out. I treasure your entire being, the breath in your body, your affectionate love, your big brown eyes, your cute smiles, your contagious laugh, your humor, your joy that lights up a room, and the peace of God that you carry in your heart. I love you more than the breath in my body!

Mom

Table of Contents

Foreword xiii
Acknowledgments xv
1. Breaking News 17
2. My Perfect Gift 25
3. Quality of Life 37
4. The Limo Ride 47
5. The Blessing 55
6. New Beginnings 65
7. Life and Death 73
8. The Battle Continues 83
9. The New Normal 93
10. Fullness of Life 103
11. God's Idea, Not Mine 115
12. The Divorce 139
13. The Word 153
14. Cool Name 167
15. Legacy 179
16. The Greatest Gift 191

Foreword

WHAT A BLESSING IT is for my wife to ask me to write the foreword to her inspiring story of her life with Paige. We were having dinner one night, and Sharon said, "I feel like God wants me to write a book about my life with Paige." Looking at her, I said, "I think you should. I believe there are a lot of people that could benefit from hearing about your life's journey with Paige."

I'm Paige's stepdad. She was eighteen years old when I came into her life. I had never spent any time with a person with special needs before I met Paige. When Sharon and I married, I was trusting God that everything would work out with Paige. Much to my surprise, the more time I spent with Paige, the more I found out how easy she is to love.

Paige is an amazing person, full of love, joy, and peace. She's kind and generous and has a genuine concern for others. Paige portrays an awesome example of unconditional love to everyone she knows. When she sees people she knows, she's always happy to see them and says their name: "There's so and so." This always makes them smile, making their day just a little brighter.

I say all of this because I do not believe that Paige's awesomeness is by chance. I believe it's the result of the deep love Sharon has shown Paige and the way she has stewarded her life, developing her into this amazing person. Sharon has also poured her faith into Paige, which is why she has become the unique and wonderful person she is today. Sharon's deep love for Paige, combined with her faith in God, has altered the trajectory of Paige's life in a very profound way. The difference is between what the professionals said Paige would be like and who Paige has miraculously become.

At first I thought this book would be helpful to parents of a child with special needs, to inspire them and help them to develop their child into a loving, joyful, and well-adjusted adult like Paige. However, while she worked on the manuscript, Sharon would read bits and pieces to me from the chapters, and her eyes would fill with tears—and so would mine as she described the almost constant battle between life and death and the victory that would follow. It seemed as if no one except Sharon had the faith that Paige would live and not die. I now understand the fullness of the story. It's more than raising a child with special needs—it's about overcoming extreme obstacles and adversity from a place of peace, with faith and deep love.

It's also about faithful stewardship, not of resources but of someone's life. Sharon has stewarded Paige's life unbelievably well. I know when that day comes and Sharon stands before our Lord, she will hear Him say, "Well done, good and faithful servant!"

This is an incredibly inspiring and courageous story about a mom and her daughter as they face and overcome seemingly no-win and very difficult life events together through faith and love. My prayer and hope are that when you read this story, you will be encouraged to have greater faith to believe God for the miraculous and be inspired to love more deeply.

Tommy

Acknowledgments

I would like to give special thanks and honor to my beloved husband, Tommy. Thank you for confirming God's idea and believing in me to do what I didn't know was possible. Thank you for your sacrificial love in making yourself available to help me with Paige so I could write. Thank you for having the "whatever it takes" attitude and cheering me on to see this book to completion. Most of all, I thank God for bringing you into my life and Paige's. You are a true gift and blessing to both of us.

All my love,
Milady

I would also like to give special thanks to my family, who were there when Paige took her first breath and have lived this story with me. Thank you all for your love and support, both physically and emotionally. Every one of you has made an impact on Paige's and my life. When I sit back and observe how much everyone loves and adores Paige, our gift, it fills my heart with an overwhelming sense of joy!

I love you all,
Sharon

Breaking News

*For You formed my inward parts;
You covered me in my mother's womb.*
Psalm 139:13

"**I don't feel like coming** to work tomorrow."
Those words had little significance to me when I spoke them, other than expressing the thought that it would be nice to have a day off from work. Little did I know I would remember them forever.

It was late Thursday afternoon at work when those words were spoken. The receptionist and I were chatting, waiting out the last few minutes before the official closing time. As I walked out after the office closed and made my way to my car, I had no idea how truthful those words were going to be. The truth was, I wasn't going back to work the next day, and life as I had known it was about to drastically change.

I've always lived a pretty good life. I'm a PK, short for preacher's kid. I was born in Guadalajara, Mexico. My parents adopted me when I was only one day old. They said I was an answer to one of their prayers, and they have always told me I was "chosen." These words carried something powerful. They made me feel good about who I am and how I was placed in this home. "I was chosen."

At the time of my birth, my parents were preparing to go to the mission field. Within a couple of years of preparation, they were sent to Africa. We lived in the Congo for two years while they taught school. I lived there with my parents and also my brother Eric, whom they adopted from Brussels, Belgium. They said he was another answer to prayer. Like me, he was "chosen." We lived in the Congo until we were evacuated due to unrest in that country.

When we came back to the States, we arrived in Texas. Over a period of years, my parents adopted two more children in Texas: my brother Teri and my sister Christi. Two more blessings and answers to prayer. We were now a family of six, each one of us "chosen." My childhood was quite normal. I attended elementary, middle, and high school all in the same area. My life was stable. I went onto college and received my degree in social work. I never had the desire to try drugs. In college I tried smoking and drinking, but neither "stuck." After college I went on to work for the Community Supervisions and Corrections Department as a probation officer, and I loved my job. This is where I was working when I spoke the words about not feeling like coming to work the next day.

I was twenty-nine years old and expecting my first baby. I was having what I thought was a normal pregnancy, just like the rest of my life. After I arrived home that evening, I went into the kitchen and made dinner. Then my husband and I pulled out the TV trays to eat dinner in the den and watch a favorite TV show. I was sitting on the couch enjoying the show when out of nowhere I felt a sudden burst of water start to flow from my body. *Oh no!* I thought. *What's going on here?* I knew something wasn't right. It wasn't time for me to give birth. I was only thirty-one weeks pregnant.

Jumping up from the couch, I headed toward the bathroom while my husband called my doctor. As I ran, water continued to flow from my body. *There's no stopping this!* It being my first pregnancy, I wasn't quite sure what to expect. It was obvious that my water had broken, but I had no idea it would be like this. *What I'm experiencing appears to be excessive. I'm not sure this is considered normal.* I assumed at some point the water would stop flowing, but it didn't.

I knew I needed medical attention for what was happening, but I just stayed in the bathroom until we received instructions from the doctor. I could hear my husband speaking with the person on call—it sounded like they were going to contact my doctor. Within minutes, the telephone rang. I listened and could hear from the conversation that my doctor was going to meet us at the hospital.

With my purse and a couple of towels in hand, I made a mad dash toward the car. Although I moved quickly, I wasn't experiencing any fear or concern. Instead, I felt perplexed and surprised by it all.

As I climbed into the car, I placed a towel on the passenger seat. It didn't take long for the water to soak through the towel. *Where's all of this water coming from?* It was as if there were an endless, reproducing supply of water. I couldn't get this off of my mind, and then I realized, *I probably need to let some people know what's going on!* I'd never gone through this before, so I didn't know the drill, but it seemed like everyone needed to share in the "good news"! Using a portable telephone (there were no cell phones yet), I began calling family members and informing them about the current state of my body and where we were headed. There was an element of surprise that quickly turned to excitement from everyone. No one was experiencing fear throughout any of this.

It took us less than thirty minutes to reach the hospital. When my husband and I arrived, a couple of nurses came out to the car to meet us. I was eager to see them, but I wasn't as calm as they were. By now, water had been coming out of my body for almost an hour, and it seemed like I was more concerned about this flow of water than anyone else. They asked me to get into a wheelchair and calmly took me to a birthing room, where they began running a series of tests. I knew there was something not right inside of me, but I never thought there was anything wrong with my baby.

"Your baby's in distress!"

I barely processed these words before I heard, "You're going to surgery. We need to do a C-section."

What? Surgery? What's going on? I don't understand any of this. I've had a normal pregnancy. My sonogram didn't reveal any problems. Why is this all happening? There has to be a mistake.

It seemed as if words were flying through the air—"Your baby's in distress. The baby's heart rate is dropping. There's a fifty-fifty chance your baby will survive."

I heard the words, but I was speechless.

The birthing room quickly turned into an emergency room. Everyone was moving quickly, talking among themselves and telling me what was going to happen. Acutely aware that the atmosphere had changed, I couldn't do anything. Everything was out of my control. I didn't have a choice. An X-ray machine arrived, and someone gave me a shot in my back, causing a chill in my spine.

At 10:33 p.m. I heard a baby's cry, followed by a doctor's voice saying, "It's a girl!" My husband and I had chosen not to know the sex ahead of time. We wanted to be surprised.

When I heard these words, I knew: *I have a daughter, and she's alive! I hear her crying, so she must be okay. The doctor's said fifty-fifty, so this must be the fifty that made it!*

The nurses called out her birth weight: "She weighs three pounds, two point five ounces."

A little small, but this seems like a pretty good birth weight given how early she is.

I assumed that everything was going to be okay. Why wouldn't it be? This was how my life had always been. I've always had a good life. The nurses continued talking—about my baby.

"Can I see her?" I asked. "I want to see what she looks like."

"Of course you can" was the reply. The nurse brought her to the side of my bed, all wrapped up in a blanket. I leaned over and glanced at her, but I didn't get to hold or even touch her. They took her away from me quickly, and we were no longer in the same room. I still wasn't afraid or disturbed; I had peace. I heard her cry. I heard her voice—and her voice was strong!

In an instant, the room began to fill with medical staff. One of the doctors spoke up. "Your daughter was having difficulty breathing, so we took her to the Neonatal Intensive Care Unit [NICU]. We wanted to do further testing."

Further testing? What do they mean by this? There's nothing wrong with her.

"We've discovered she has some ribs that are fused together," he continued, "and she has TE Fistula."

My husband and I turned to look at each other. *Fused ribs? This doesn't make sense. I've never heard of this, but I can handle fused ribs—she's alive. But I'm not quite sure what he means by TE Fistula. I don't know what that is. I'm sure it's going to be an easy thing to fix though.*

The next words answered my question.

"Your daughter's esophagus didn't attach to her stomach. Surgery is the only way to repair this, and we have to do it immediately so that she's able to receive nourishment. We've scheduled this surgery for tomorrow."

Surgery? How can this be? Should I be concerned? Once again, I didn't have a choice. My daughter didn't have a choice either.

I might not have had a choice about the surgery, but I chose not to be concerned or worried, thinking, *The surgeon's going to do this surgery, fix the problem, and everything's going to be fine.* What I didn't know was that this surgery would not fix the problem; instead, it would create additional problems for our daughter.

By this time, some of our immediate family had arrived, and they were getting updates. My parents didn't live in the area, so after making the two-hour drive into town, my mom arrived at 1:30 a.m. When she arrived, she found me in a room where I was by myself.

After I received all of the updates from the doctors, they moved me away from the maternity unit. "It's insensitive to keep you in a unit where other moms have their babies in the same room with them," they had said.

I wasn't sure if this made me feel better or not. Where they moved me felt sterile and isolated. As I laid there in silence, I had more time to think. *I don't understand any of this. This isn't how I dreamed having a baby was going to be. Why am I having to go through this? Why is my story not looking like everyone else's? How can I possibly comprehend what just happened?* When my mom walked through the door, I was feeling very alone.

I knew I had just given birth by C-section to a baby girl. I knew I'd dreamed about this baby for months, maybe all of my life. I'd spent time imagining what life would be like being a new mom and often wondering what kind of mom I'd be. *Am I going to be a good mom? Am I going to be the best mom for my child? Is it going to be easy? Am I going to know what to do?* I'd dreamed about what our family would look like having a new addition. *How are our lives going to change? I can only imagine the joy and happiness this baby's going to bring!* Although we chose not to know the sex, we did have a name for her—Paige!

I woke up the next morning and casually thought, *Today's Friday.* And then it registered. *Friday! I'm supposed to go to work today!* I suddenly remembered the words I'd spoken just yesterday: "I don't feel like coming to work tomorrow." Those words had now become a reality. A reality that was in its early stages of unfolding. A reality I could never have anticipated. A reality that would change my life forever.

My Perfect Gift

Every good gift and every perfect gift is from above.
James 1:17

THE PAIN'S ALMOST UNBEARABLE—I held my breath and quickly put my hand across the stitches on my stomach. *How could I have forgotten about this?* It was tempting to get back into bed, but I was on mission. I didn't care that I had just had a C-section; I wanted to see my baby. *I'm not going to let this pain stop me.* I could've asked for a wheelchair, but I chose to walk from my private room to the NICU.

My daughter's having surgery today, and I want to be with her.

I hadn't seen her since they took her away from me. Now she was in an incubator hooked up to a lot of machines with various tubes coming in and out of her. She looked tiny, with a head full of dark brown hair, and was kind of long and skinny. I thought she looked fine. *She just needs to gain some weight.*

I waited beside the incubator taking in all of the sounds of the machines—the beeps, the drips, the alarms—gazing at all of them, trying to find out their purpose and what all the numbers meant. Between 4:30 and 5:30 p.m., the medical staff arrived to take Paige into surgery—the surgery where the surgeon would be attaching her esophagus to her stomach so that she could have nourishment.

Until now, I'd remained quite calm.

As I watched the medical staff, I saw their pace increase, and they began hustling around Paige. Sitting there quietly, the significance of what happened the day before began to sink in. *I've given birth to a baby that wasn't full-term. She's not even twenty-four hours old, and she's about to go into surgery.* A weightiness of grief and sadness descended upon me. My eyes filled with tears. I tried to hold them back, to be strong, but the grief and sadness wasn't going away. I struggled to keep myself together.

Attempting to be brave, I took a deep breath as they wheeled her away.

"We're going to take good care of her."

Those words echoed in my head. I wanted them to be true. *Please take good care of her.*

Then they directed my husband and me to a waiting room filled with family and friends. Although I was comforted by seeing everyone, it was difficult to engage in conversation. I kept looking at the clock to see how much time has passed. If I wasn't looking at the clock, I was listening for the phone to ring because it was my way of staying connected with Paige.

After waiting a very long two hours, the surgeon appeared at the door, and my heart leaped, anticipating his words.

"The surgery went well."

I let out a deep sigh of relief. Those were the sweetest words to hear, what we'd hoped for. *Everything's going to be okay, just like my life has always been.* But before I could take another breath, I received a devastating blow.

"During surgery we discovered another issue."

What? Another issue? He had my full attention.

"There's an issue with Paige's heart, which will require at least one surgery."

Her heart?

In hearing those words, it was as if an arrow pierced my own heart. The room began to spin. I heard the doctor's voice speaking words, but I didn't understand even one of them. It seemed as if all of his words were moving in slow motion. I was no longer thinking about Paige's survival—now I was wondering how I was going to survive.

Paige was two days old, and she was recovering from surgery. All was not well. She was in critical condition. She needed to have her first blood transfusion. She was pale and lethargic. Everything we were experiencing was all so new, and fear was beginning to set in. Our family and friends didn't know what to do, yet no one wanted to leave.

It had only been thirty-six hours since Paige's birth, yet it seemed like my life was spinning out of control. Not only my life, but me—and who I'd known myself to be. My mind now began to fill with thoughts, words, and ideas that were causing confusion and uncertainty. I couldn't seem to keep the barrage of thoughts away. The atmosphere of peace I had carried just days ago when I had no worries or concerns now changed to feelings of great unease. My entire body was restless. I couldn't seem to sit still, yet on this day, a moment occurred when all of the unease stilled—a moment that will be imprinted on my heart forever.

> Today I walked into the hospital room and saw you lying in the ICU incubator. You were lying on your side and your eyes were open. This is the first time that our eyes have connected with each other. There was nothing ordinary about this moment. It was powerful. There was something about seeing your eyes that caused me to draw near to you.
>
> When I looked into your big brown eyes, I saw a person. It's not that I didn't know you were a person, my baby, my daughter.

There was something different about this moment. It was in this moment that I *saw you.*

There's a person in there. A person who has feelings. A person who has thoughts and emotions. This person has no idea what's going on in her life. I don't even know if this person knows who I am.

You were looking deep into my eyes. You were connecting with me through your eyes. It was as if you were talking to me without saying a word. I don't know what you were trying to say to me, but I do know that it was in that moment I became so in love with you. Yet at the same time I was so afraid to love you for fear of the pain it might cause me. I was so overwhelmed that I needed to look away so you wouldn't see my tears.

But when I tried to explain this encounter to the others, they didn't understand my tears, they didn't understand how hard it was for me to look into your eyes. They called what I experienced with you "a sweet moment." Under any other set of circumstances, I might have experienced it that way. But this encounter kind of made me want to run away. It wasn't that I wanted to run away from you—I wanted to run away from the real possibility that my heart could be deeply hurt, more than I could bear.

Thoughts swirled through my head: *Where do I go from here? How do I navigate through this? I have a little person who's depending on me, yet I don't know if I can be here for her. I might get hurt.* At that point, I didn't have any answers.

Four days after giving birth by C-section, they told me I was ready to leave the hospital. But I wasn't ready to leave.

One of the nurses brought me a cart to load up all of the gifts I'd received, and I walked around the room picking up each flower arrangement, each stuffed animal, and each card, placing them on the cart. *This isn't what I thought having a baby was going to be like. None of it has gone as I've planned or dreamed about. It seems as if everyone's making decisions for me, and I don't have a say. I'm doing the next thing that's put in front of me, but it doesn't feel right. I'm going home, and I don't have a baby with me. This is all wrong.*

With everything loaded into the car, my husband and I drove home. The drive was silent. Then before I knew it, we were pulling into the garage. Still recovering from my C-section, I moved very slowly and carefully as I walked into the house. I hadn't been here since my water broke, just a few days before. As I stepped into the house from the garage, I walked right into the den where it all began.

Memories of that evening flooded my mind.

I saw myself sitting on the couch eating dinner and watching television. I relived the memories of my water breaking and my husband and I hustling around the house. Now the house felt lifeless and empty. The room looked the same, but the life that had been there was missing.

I continued walking through the house, making my way to the baby's bedroom. I stood in the doorway and stared into the room. I saw rays of sunshine penetrating the sheer curtains and filling the entire room with beautiful promises.

More memories came pouring into my head. I was remembering the day my husband and I had set aside to paint our baby's bedroom. We wanted everything to be perfect! Every time we dipped the paint roller or the paintbrush into the paint, we each shared what we thought life would be like with our new addition, how perfect we thought it would be. After we painted the walls and trim, we placed a border of baby ducks around the top of the room. Then when everything was in place, we stood back and inspected our labor of love. It was a white-picket-fence kind of day.

I continued staring into the room, but now I realized that picket-fence day had been wishful imagination. I saw paint on the walls and trim, and I noticed the border of baby ducks around the top of the room, but that was all. There was no furniture, and there was no baby. Paige was not here.

Early the next morning the telephone rang, and a man who identified himself as one of the neonatologists from the hospital was calling about Paige. I could barely listen to the next words that came out of his mouth.

"We performed a CT scan that revealed Paige suffered a brain hemorrhage after birth." Then he quickly added, "This most likely occurred during the surgery. It's not uncommon in preemies. We give these types of bleeds a rating, between one and four. We've given this bleed a rating of two. Many times there's no evidence of this type of bleed."

I listened, stunned, not believing I was hearing these words. *Does this mean she has brain damage?*

The next day I was still processing this information when the telephone rang again. I knew this voice. It was the same voice that had called yesterday, the neonatologist calling from the hospital: "A blood test has revealed that Paige has a problem with her chromosomes. She has an extra piece of a chromosome. You and your husband need to come in for testing of your chromosomes."

I listened, and I heard what he said, but this time it felt like my insides were unraveling. *Paige is only one week old—how can there be more problems?*

Twenty-four hours later, my husband and I were sitting with a doctor and a representative from the Child Study Center, and we were giving blood. After we were done, they led us over to a table where we all sat down. The doctor opened a folder and handed us photocopies of what looked like DNA strands. For the first time, I was seeing photos of Paige's chromosomes.

Sure enough, there it is in the photo, an extra piece of a chromosome.

I sat there looking at the photo that made no sense to me. I had taken biology in school, but that didn't mean I knew the significance of this extra piece of chromosome. I had no idea, but I listened as the doctor explained four different scenarios.

This is all new and foreign to me. What's she saying? What does this mean? What does this mean for Paige? How could a chromosome that's so tiny cause so many problems? The atmosphere seemed so surreal. *This has to be someone else's life. Or a bad dream, one I'm going to wake up from.*

However, I knew it wasn't a dream. I was awake, this was very real, and it was my reality.

Although difficult to hear, I knew that the representative at the Child Study Center was just doing her job. Before leaving, she suggested my husband and I attend a support group called "Our Special Children." I got the impression she thought it would be a good idea for us to get used to having a child with special needs. She gave us the date for the next meeting, which happened to be the next week, and we decided to go.

The location of this meeting was near the hospital, which made it convenient to be near Paige. As we drove up, I looked at the front of the building and sat there wondering, *What's inside this building that has to do with us?* We didn't know what to expect, but once inside we walked around until we found the one room full of people. As I looked around, I assumed everyone there had a child with special needs. The people seemed friendly enough. The chairs were in a circle so we could see everyone as we shared our stories. The meeting started, and one by one everyone had a turn to tell their story. Many of these parents shared their challenges and the uncertainties they were facing.

Sitting there listening, I took in their stories and their concerns, and I heard sadness in their voices. At the same time, I was wondering, *What does all of this have to do with me? What do their stories mean for me?*

This sharing lasted about an hour, and I was feeling a bit overwhelmed by it. As we walked out, more uncertainty filled me. *What's ahead in our future? What's our story going to look like?*

About two weeks later, the results returned from the chromosome testing. Once again I heard the telephone ring, though I didn't think anything about the call. This time I didn't recognize the voice, but it was someone from the hospital calling to give us the test results: "Mom is the one who carries the extra piece of a chromosome."

Those words sent me into shock. *I don't understand. How can I carry this extra piece of a chromosome and have no evidence of it in my body?*

The caller went on to explain. Although I had an extra piece of a chromosome, the extra piece in my body attached itself to another chromosome in my body. This was why I didn't have any of the issues Paige had.

He continued, "If this extra piece would have attached to another chromosome in Paige's body, she would be like you and have no evidence. Unlike you, the extra piece of chromosome didn't know where to attach."

By now I was feeling extremely upset, and when I hung up the telephone, I broke into deep sobbing tears. My once-normal life—once so in control—had become uncontrollably shattered.

One bad report after another filled the first two and a half weeks of Paige's life, and I knew that all of the problems in her body were only decreasing the odds of her ever coming home. I needed some time to be alone, to process everything. And the only idea that came to my mind was to go and see my parents who lived about two hours away. It was away, but not too far away—it seemed like a good place to go.

My Perfect Gift

I called my parents and gave them the update, and I asked if I could come out. Both of them wanted to help in any way they possibly could, so my husband took off from work to be with Paige at the hospital, and I headed to East Texas.

I didn't know what would happen while I was there. There was no agenda. It just seemed like this was what I needed to do. My parents live on over sixty acres of land, away from the busyness of the city. It's a peaceful place. They call their home "Canyon Pines." Aspens and pine trees dot the land, and there are walking trails throughout. Their modest house looks out onto a manmade pond with a fishing pier and a paddle boat in it. There's something about being with my parents and on this land that brings me feelings of comfort. Although I was looking for comfort, I had no idea that what I was about to experience would be a major turning point in my life.

I'd been raised in church all of my life but had very little knowledge of the Bible. I did know the basic children's stories taught in Sunday school, but I didn't know a lot about Scripture. I'm sure I'd read a few verses over the years, but I didn't have any favorites, nor did I have any understanding about their meaning. However, during this time in East Texas, God found me.

Early one morning I decided to go jogging on the trails. I loved being outside and was enjoying the crisp, cool morning air when I began having unusual thoughts. I kept hearing the same thing over and over.

Where are these thoughts coming from? They sound like Scripture.
Every good gift comes from above.
Every good gift comes from above.
Every good gift comes from above.

The words seemed to come out of nowhere and got my full attention. I stopped in the middle of the path and didn't move. *What's going on here? I haven't heard these words before. Where are they coming from? What do they mean?* I sat down on a nearby tree stump and pondered them.

I know that God is above. Do these words have to do with God? I couldn't think of anything other than this. *These thoughts must have to do with God. If every good gift comes from above, then every good gift must come from God.* It was as if God was trying to speak to me. I'd never had God speak to me before, but if He had, I hadn't known it. And it had never been like this!

I was on full alert now. *What are You trying to say to me, God? What are You saying? If every good gift comes from God, then what gift have You given me?* I waited to see if I would hear anything else. *Paige—is Paige the gift? Is that what You're saying?* If Paige is the gift, then she must be a good gift because I was hearing that every good gift comes from God.

Something started to happen inside of me. I began to have this knowing. I began to know that those words I was hearing were meant for *me*. I couldn't stop thinking about those words, and I couldn't stop thinking about God giving good gifts.

I could feel excitement rising in me—excitement I couldn't contain about the gift God had given me. It rose up in me like a fountain, and in those moments, I began to see Paige differently. I started seeing Paige as a gift.

Something else was happening too. Not only did I now know that Paige was a gift, but an intensity of joy was coming upon me—the hopelessness and despair had lifted. I had energy again, and I was feeling more like I'd known myself to be. Something was definitely changing.

Energized with excitement, I could hardly wait to get back to the house to tell my parents what happened and get back home to see "my gift"—the perfect gift God had given me.

My Perfect Gift

Every good gift and every perfect gift is from above. (James 1:17)

Paige must be perfect!

I'd never seen this Scripture before, and I didn't even know if it existed in the Bible. However, it was in that moment, in the middle of the trail, when I felt like God was speaking to me. Paige's birth was beginning to have purpose. Somehow, what I'd just heard had caused me to feel chosen, honored, and empowered.

Chosen: I was chosen to be Paige's mom. *Out of all of the people God could have given Paige to, He chose me.* I was chosen.

Honored: *Since Paige was going to be born into this world, God wanted me to take care of her. God must trust me.* It was as if God was looking upon me with high respect, giving me the privilege of taking care of someone with different needs.

Empowered: These words from God gave me a different perspective. I'd been given God's perspective on my situation, and it strengthened me. I felt encouraged. I felt more equipped to face my reality.

Something definitely had changed for me. I had a new set of lenses. I had a new outlook on my current circumstances. I now saw Paige as a gift. A good gift. And I saw her through the lens of perfection. *She's perfect! No matter what she looks like on the outside, today or in the days to come, she's still perfect.*

I could hardly wait to tell everyone that God had spoken to me. I wanted to share my good news! I wanted to let them know how God felt about me and how He felt about Paige. He had "chosen me" to be Paige's mom. He "trusted me." She's "my gift" from God.

And no matter what, "She's perfect!"

Quality of Life

*For I know the thoughts that I think toward you, says the Lord,
thoughts of peace and not of evil, to give you a future and a hope.*
Jeremiah 29:11

THE EXPERIENCE I HAD in East Texas was a major turning point in my life. As far as I was concerned, I had discovered the answer to all of the problems we were facing. I now knew Paige was a gift; however it didn't take me long to realize that other people didn't have this same revelation. I had only been gone a couple of days, but upon my return to the hospital to see Paige, I faced a lot of resistance. I had to shake off words spoken as well as pessimistic attitudes. I hadn't been expecting this, yet I knew I wasn't going to allow these things to steal my joy.

Paige was born in late February, toward the end of a Texas winter. We were now two weeks into March and getting closer to spring. I couldn't help but notice how bright the sun was shining and how cool and crisp the air felt. It was all so refreshing and encouraging to me because I was noticing these things again. Until now, I hadn't been able to look beyond our circumstances to experience life around me. Aware of the bounce in my step and the unexplained energy and joy in my heart, I walked through the front doors of the hospital ready to start living!

I'm ready to start living life with my beautiful gift!

The hospital had become our home away from home, since my husband and I had been there every day, and I'd found that I felt more at peace when I was there with Paige. I got to hold her hand, talk to her, and play music. Until now, no one had been allowed to hold her. But this was about to change.

Paige is three weeks old today, and I get to hold her.

I wasn't sure what to expect, but I knew it was a significant moment. They told us only one person could hold Paige today, and the unanimous decision was that I would be the one to hold her first. I had carried her inside me for seven months and given birth to her, but I'd never held her in my arms, not even for a second.

One of the requirements before entering the ICU is to put a gown on and wash your hands for three minutes. This process seemed so much longer today, since I knew I was just moments away from getting to hold Paige. I couldn't get there fast enough. After finishing the three-minute wash and drying my hands, I felt ready to walk through the doors—the doors that would take me to Paige. My husband had a camera and a camcorder with him to capture this special moment, not only with our daughter but with our gift!

We walked straight over to Paige, and I noticed that someone had placed a wooden rocking chair beside her incubator. The nursing staff came over to greet us, knowing that today was special.

"Are you ready?" a nurse asked.

"I'm ready!" She didn't have to ask me twice. Seated in the wooden rocking chair, I positioned my arms to receive Paige—"my gift."

It didn't make for an easy transfer into my arms because Paige was hooked up to a lot of tubes and medical equipment. With great anticipation, I watched the nurses move all of the tubing and equipment around—tubes and wires seemed everywhere. After they moved everything out of the way, they lifted Paige out of the incubator and placed her in my arms.

Once her tiny body touched mine, I experienced the reality of what I'd been missing. In that moment, I was overwhelmed by the magnitude of closeness I felt with her. It was a completely new feeling to me. No doubt we'd had such a moment when our eyes first connected, but there was something about holding her in my arms that removed any doubt I was her mom.

She needs me. She needs to be this close to me as much as possible. She needs to know how loved she is.

As I held my daughter, I was being filled up. I felt the warmth we were sharing and knew bonding was taking place. We'd connected again, this time outside of the womb. My heart was filling with gratefulness for this little girl in my arms—named Paige.

It wasn't long before the nurses began gathering up the tubes and positioning them back into the incubator. They'd informed us that she could only be out of the incubator for five minutes. Although those five minutes passed quickly, I knew in my heart things were changing.

I have a great attitude, a new set of lenses to see my life through—and my life with Paige!

It was hard to believe that in one week Paige would be one month old. So much had happened during that time. I had given birth unexpectedly. Paige had received multiple medical diagnoses. And anguish had penetrated my heart over and over again. Most importantly, I'd had an encounter with God that helped me see this situation with a new set of lenses.

Paige is a gift!
She is my gift!
She has been entrusted into my care!
I was chosen out of many!

About one week after getting to hold Paige, we received a call from the Child Study Center.

The representative said, "Paige will have mental problems."

I heard those words just like I'd heard all the other words, but for some reason this information didn't have any effect on me.

In addition to the call from the Child Study Center, one of the doctors called, telling us they'd discovered another problem.

"Further testing has revealed that fluid is filling inside Paige's head." When I didn't respond, he said, "It's actually inside her brain. This fluid isn't supposed to be there." He called it hydrocephalus.

I didn't know what to make of this new information, but I wasn't moved by any of it.

A week later, the phone rang again. I wondered if it was the hospital, but this time the thought didn't upset me. Sure enough, it was the main neonatologist assigned to Paige.

"I'm calling to set up a conference with you at 3 p.m. today," he said. "You'll be meeting with me and one of the nurses in the unit. We'd like to talk with you and your husband about a decision that needs to be made. This decision concerns continued surgical procedures for Paige."

What in the world am I hearing? What does this mean? What are they asking us to do?

Within a few short hours, my husband and I were sitting in a room with Dr. A. and Nurse J. It was a simple room with a table and a few chairs—no pictures on the walls or anything that would make you feel warm and hopeful. With no delay, they got right to the point of this meeting. I basically heard the same words as spoken over the telephone. The only difference was this conversation was face to face.

The doctor said, "It's our professional medical opinion that further intervention would only prolong a life that is not going to be of good quality." And then he said something about "poor quality of life."

Poor quality of life? Those words stood out to me the most, resonating in my head—"poor quality of life."

I was stunned. *How can a doctor who helps people get well say that they don't want to do anything more to help? Have they asked anyone else to make this decision? Or are we the first? I've never heard of anything like this before.*

They asked us to give this some thought and then give them an answer. Without a word, my husband and I left that meeting, and I went straight to see Paige.

Entering through the doors of the ICU, I walked up to the incubator that Paige was in and looked into her bed. *She doesn't look good.* Although she'd gained some weight and now weighed in at four pounds, her body was very puffy, and she appeared distressed. Her face and eyes were really contorted. *Something doesn't look right.* It was difficult to see her this way, and everything I saw brought me sadness. I continued looking at her while the words about having a "poor quality of life" resonated in my head. Leaning over, I gave Paige a hug and a kiss and told her I'd be back.

As I walked away, thoughts clamored in my head. *We have a big decision to make. The doctors are looking to us to decide Paige's future. I can't comprehend the fact that we've been asked to make this decision. Who's to say what quality of life is? I want to know the answer to this question.*

I set out to find the answer.

I wasn't sure where to go first, but then I thought about the library. We didn't have internet back then, so the library seemed like a good place to start. I began pulling any book off the shelves that mentioned quality of life. After gathering several books, I sat down at a table and opened the first one. Flipping through its pages, I saw photos for the first time of children with chromosome issues and what they looked like. I sat there reading about their lives and the limitations they face. I kept looking, and I kept reading.

As I tried to comprehend the meaning of these photos, I thought, *We don't know what Paige's life is going to look like. Who's to say that her life is going to look like the children in these photos? Who's to say what she's going to be able to do or not do? Who's supposed to determine what quality of life is? The doctors? Or God?* The thoughts that had swirled through my head only days earlier came flooding into my head. *Paige is a gift. She is a gift from God.*

Had I already forgotten how excited I was that God trusted me with her life? Had I already forgotten that God had chosen me from the multitude? Had I already forgotten how these thoughts strengthened and encouraged me? Had I already forgotten how empowered these words made me feel? Had I already forgotten how honored I was to be Paige's mom?

As I sat there reflecting, something was rising up inside me again, and I began to feel strength come back into my body. I began to feel peace in my heart. I began to feel victorious. I began to feel like I had a say. I began to feel like I had a voice. Yes! I had a voice over Paige's life, and my voice chose to say:

God has given me Paige.
She is a gift.
She is perfect!
Who are we to say what quality of life looks like?
Who are we to make this decision?
God is going to have the final say over her life.
Yes! God is going to have the final say!

I'd found what I was looking for, and I was finished at the library. I replaced all the books and walked out. Once again, I felt hope rising inside of me over Paige's life, all of my burdens removed. It was late, so I wasn't able to go back and see Paige. *I'll see her tomorrow.*

The next morning, I awoke with a grateful heart. I'd made peace with what the doctors wanted my husband and me to do. We both agreed—and there's power in agreement—that God would have the final say over Paige's life. I couldn't wait to see her.

By now I knew the layout of the hospital, the fastest way to park, and the easiest way to get to the ICU. As I walked into the unit, the nursing staff approached me with surprising news. Paige had taken herself off the ventilator during the night. Until now, she'd been on one to help her breathe. The nurses told me she'd done this around midnight. To everyone's surprise, Paige was actually doing very well.

What should I make of this news?

I went over to the bed to see for myself and couldn't believe my eyes. Within twenty-four hours, Paige had changed. Now when I looked at her, she looked very comfortable. She'd already lost some of the excess fluid in her body and looked good. I began to wonder, *Is this a sign?*

Although I didn't know much about God and signs, that's what came to my mind. It was obvious that Paige was better, and for the first time since her birth I heard her cry.

She took herself off the ventilator. Maybe she's trying to tell us something. Maybe she's telling us that she's very much alive! There was no denying that something out of the ordinary had happened. I knew it, and so did everyone else.

Paige was breathing on her own! We had something positive to hold onto. However, we received a gentle reminder that Paige needed another surgery to help correct the hydrocephalus that had developed in her brain.

Here's a little background: The hydrocephalus had developed from a brain bleed after Paige was born. Being a preemie, her brain was still developing, and the blood vessels were still growing rapidly. Most likely, the hemorrhage occurred the day after Paige was born, when she went into the surgery that attached her esophagus to her stomach. The bleed received a number two rating. No one ever expected to see any evidence, yet we did. Spinal fluid was building up inside of Paige's brain and causing pressure that could lead to further brain damage. She needed to have a shunt put into her brain so the spinal fluid could drain to another part of her body, where it could reabsorb.

This newer development was one of the reasons the doctors talked with us about not doing any further medical intervention. During this meeting they also reminded us that every major organ in Paige's body was compromised, and almost every specialist was following her.

We knew that the doctors were waiting for our answer about further medical intervention, but before we ever had the discussion with Doctor A and Nurse J, this surgery was already on the calendar for the first week of April. We didn't say a word.

The day of the surgery came, and they placed the shunt into Paige's brain. The surgeon said, "She tolerated it." Kind of empty, unsympathetic words to me. The next few days were busy doing smaller procedures, and other doctors stopped by to check on her. The main neonatologist was not calling, and we found ourselves happy about this lack of communication. For the first time since Paige was born, things seemed to be more "normal." She still needed to have a heart surgery, and she wasn't ready to come home, but things felt more peaceful.

We didn't get to experience this feeling of "normal" for very long though—maybe two weeks before the telephone rang again. It was the hospital calling. You'd think I'd have been used to this by now, but I wasn't. Each time they called, I felt like I had to prepare myself for what I was about to hear.

It was one of the neonatologists again, and this time he said, "The shunt's not working. A head sonogram showed fluid on Paige's brain and possible clots."

Although he didn't come right out and say it, I could sense that he didn't recommend this surgery. After hanging up the phone, I just stood there. This call bothered me. I wasn't sure what to think about everything—the doctor, his words, or the fact Paige would have to undergo yet another surgery. *We just put her through this surgery, and it didn't work.* My husband and I both knew that no one supported us in continuing medical intervention. The only thing we both knew in that moment was "God is going to have the final say over Paige's life."

I informed my husband of this new information. We intended to request surgery.

At that time, I was sharing an office with another probation officer, so I waited until I was by myself to make the phone call. Taking a deep breath, I dialed the hospital number. When the nurse came to the phone, I could hear my voice shaking, and it was all I could do not to cry. The nurse knew I was having a difficult time speaking and conveying what I wanted to say. When I was finally able to speak, I said, "I know you don't understand, and no one agrees that we should put Paige through any more surgeries, but my husband and I are giving the directive to have this surgery done."

No one said a word.

Paige did have the surgery. During the procedure, the surgeon found a clot that was located inside of the shunt, so he was able to clean it out instead of having to replace the entire shunt. In our minds, this was fantastic news!

However, that evening when I went to see Paige, one of the many doctors assigned to her was in the ICU. He was doing his rounds and stopped by her bed, where he found me. I was super excited that there was an easy explanation why the shunt hadn't been working instead of Paige's body rejecting it, and I couldn't help but express my excitement to him. However, not only didn't he share my enthusiasm, he met it with resistance and replied with discouraging words.

"I don't recommend doing further surgeries."

I couldn't believe what I'd just heard. *Those words are still out there. They haven't been forgotten, and now they're coming from another doctor. I'm believing for Paige to live, and others are believing for her to die.*

The Limo Ride

For God is not the author of confusion but of peace.
1 Corinthians 14:33

DURING THE NIGHT, I kept mentally replaying what I'd heard from the doctor, which caused me to toss and turn all night. I didn't get much sleep. At the crack of dawn, I was back at the hospital. But when I walked into the room where Paige had been for two months, she wasn't there. My heart skipped a beat. Keeping the feeling of shock at bay, I asked the nurses where Paige was and they told me that she'd been moved upstairs.

Upstairs? What does that mean? Why did they move her upstairs?

I bypassed the elevator and climbed the stairwell to get to her. When I found Paige, she was no longer in an incubator—she was now in a baby bed. She looked beautiful, yet my mind was trying to interpret what was going on.

Why is Paige in a baby bed? What's going on here?

I asked the nurse, "Why has Paige been moved?"

"We moved Paige upstairs," she said, "so you can have some quiet time with her."

Quiet time? I'm not going to receive these words over Paige's life. God is going to have the final say.

Within a few days, Paige wasn't doing well, yet during my lunch hour I found myself shopping for her. I'd only been back to work for two weeks. I purchased a couple of preemie outfits. I could hardly wait to see Paige so I could put one on her!

I was beaming upon my return to the NICU, and the nurse assigned to Paige took notice of my purchases.

"She's so sick," the nurse said.

I heard these words, but I also heard what she didn't say: "Don't get your hopes up." Without any hesitation, I replied, "Well, she's going to look good while she gets better!" *Why can't anyone be on our side?*

I wasn't in denial. I saw what everyone else was seeing. Outwardly, Paige was not getting better. She was having setbacks, and ultimately the shunt wasn't working again. They were measuring the circumference of her head daily, and it kept increasing in size. Since it already had been established that "God is going to have the final say over Paige's life," my husband and I knew we were going to authorize yet another surgery. We were determined to give Paige every possible chance of survival. Although not everyone agreed, everyone knew she couldn't survive without it.

They scheduled surgery, and that day I was up early, ready to make my daily phone call to the hospital. By now, I knew all too well that shift change was at 7:00 a.m., so I waited until 7:15 a.m. to call.

"Good morning. I'm calling to check on Paige. Can you give me the measurement of her head?"

I could hear the nurse flipping through the chart, and she said nonchalantly, "The measurement is 38.5."

My eyes got big when I heard this number. *This measurement is significant. If I've heard correctly, it means that the size of her head has gone down.* I asked again to be sure I'd heard correctly.

She repeated the same number, and, yes, I'd heard correctly. This measurement was less than the day before, indicating that the shunt was working! Ready to do a happy dance, I knew I needed to make some phone calls. *We need to stop the surgery!*

When I couldn't reach one doctor, I called another, leaving messages along the way. I didn't know if anyone else had noticed, but I was determined to bring this news to everyone's attention. They needed to know that the size of Paige's head had gone down. I believed this was another sign. It was as if we'd been told not to do this surgery because she didn't need it. The surgeon canceled the surgery, which filled me with an overwhelming sense of relief.

By evening, I was standing by Paige's bed. Just then, one of her doctors came into the room and stood beside me. It was the same doctor whose words had caused me to toss and turn all night.

"I can't believe what happened today," he said. "I don't know if I'd call it an act of God, but you must have lived an awful good life."

I was a little stunned, not believing the words I'd just heard. Standing there in amazement with happiness in my heart, I realized that one of the medical staff had finally spoken some positive words.

The doctors never asked us again for a response to their question regarding medical intervention. I believe they began to know what our answer was always going to be, and Paige continued to get better.

Paige was now three months old, and we were more than ready for her to come home, yet she still needed another surgery, a surgery to repair her heart. We met with the heart surgeon who would perform the operation, and she went over the entire procedure and the risk.

This surgery made me nervous and excited and scared at the same time. It was exciting because Paige was finally healthy enough to have it. But it was scary in all sorts of ways. I couldn't keep myself from thinking about the possibility that we'd come all this way and could still lose her. I also remembered we'd experienced setbacks from surgeries, so I hoped we wouldn't run into any more problems. There was no getting around this surgery, Paige couldn't come home without it. The only way to move was forward.

In preparing us, the anesthesiologist told us that there are fifteen minutes during the surgery that are the most critical—when they deflate the lung and move it over. I believed he was telling us everything we needed to know, yet this information was only making it more difficult. They took Paige into surgery at 11:20 a.m. It was extremely hard to give her a hug and a kiss and say the words "I love you." Each time she went into surgery, my heart longed to see her alive again.

After watching Paige go through the double doors, my husband and I made our way toward the all-too-familiar waiting room, now filled with our family and friends. It's hard waiting, knowing that your loved one is in surgery. Everyone tries to help make the time go by faster with light conversation. Emotions are heightened so you really can't go very deep. No one left the room until we saw the surgeon walk through the door at 4:00 p.m. and say, "She's okay." Paige was on her way to recovery, and I wanted to lay eyes on her.

But when I saw Paige, she had cuts all over her body. *What's this?*

When I asked the nurse, she said, "They had a hard time getting an arterial line. The surgeon is concerned because it's an indication that Paige's tissues are very fragile."

Overall though, the surgeon was very pleased with the shunt's placement into her heart. Although I didn't like all of the cuts, I accepted the answer.

Now that this surgery was over, I was getting more and more excited. Things were progressing in the right direction. All of the nurses were now stopping by to see Paige, and one of the doctors who'd been so discouraging also seemed pleased. He actually said, "If we can get Paige breathing on her own, you can take her home."

My eyes lit up. No one had ever said anything to us before about the possibility of Paige coming home. This really was exciting!

As I began thinking about the real possibility of Paige coming home, I had an idea. *Paige is coming home in a limo!* I shared this with my husband, and it was unanimous.

But it wasn't over yet. In the midst of all this excitement, the doctors informed us that Paige needed yet another surgery. *Another surgery?* This news came out of nowhere. I thought we'd finished with surgeries—and, besides, somehow this news felt backward, like the tables had turned. Now the doctors were telling us that they needed to do a surgery, and I was the one who couldn't bear the thought of putting Paige through another one. *What surgery could she possibly need? I hope we didn't fix Paige all up just to have her spend the rest of her life having surgeries.*

There was no choice. "What's next?"

"Paige isn't swallowing like she should."

I knew about this, but since she'd never been given a bottle, I thought we would start there. Why surgery?

"It's more than that," they said. "She needs to have a feeding tube placed into her stomach."

A feeding tube? I've never heard of anything like this. The hospital staff showed us what this feeding tube would look like. They called it a G-button.

"She's going to eat this way," the doctor said.

Eat this way? I can't believe Paige is going to eat through her stomach. This doesn't make sense to me at all. I had strong thoughts and feelings about it, but what could I say? She couldn't come home without it.

"She'll be able to come home ten days after this surgery."

What! Ten days! We're now within ten days of Paige coming home! After four months, Paige coming home was finally becoming a reality. *Her room? It's not ready! We need to get furniture for her room.*

All of a sudden everything was happening very fast, and we weren't ready.

Even though we'd heard ten days, it was a guesstimate. Full of excitement now, everyone in the family started playing a fun game of "Who can guess the date Paige will come home?" We all put our names on the day we thought it might be.

My husband and I scheduled CPR classes, and I scheduled follow-up doctor appointments as the doctors were ordering final tests for Paige. Meanwhile, I was learning how to arrange for all the medical equipment Paige would need at home.

We're in the home stretch! Or so I thought.

Our final days came with another obstacle—something new had been found inside of Paige's brain during the final CT scan.

"There's a dark area, which we suspect is a tumor," the doctor told us. "We'd like to do a fusion dye to see if this is true."

In sheer disbelief at his words, my heart sank to the floor. *I can't believe we're this close to coming home, and now Paige may have a tumor!*

The doctor could see that I was emotionally numb. For the first time since giving birth to Paige, the neonatologist was trying to comfort me.

The following day they performed a fusion scan, but we had to wait twenty-four hours for the results. After those long hours finally passed, I called the doctor to find out the test results.

He knew why I was calling and immediately said, "The dark area is *not* a tumor! We don't know what it is. It could be old blood or tissue from a previous surgery."

The Limo Ride

He kind of lost me after "it's *not* a tumor!" because as far as I was concerned, I didn't care what it was. *This is great news! All the test results are in, and Paige is coming home!*

In my complete joy of Paige coming home, I'd forgotten the conversation I'd had with the receptionist at my job about not wanting to go to work the next day. And, as it turned out, I didn't go to work the next day. When I'd spoken those words, I had no idea I was about to give birth. Nor did I have any idea what the next four months of my life were going to look like.

Paige is four months old and she's coming home. That's all I could think about. The neonatologist who had followed Paige since she was born helped us get her dressed while we took a lot of pictures. A couple of the nurses came to see Paige.

One nurse said, "I've never seen a baby who had so many things going against them get out of here!" She was on the verge of tears. When I heard her say that, I felt chills all over my body.

We thanked everyone, said goodbye, and put Paige into her stroller. With joy in my heart, my husband and I pushed Paige toward the elevator. Once inside, my husband reached out and pushed the button for the first floor. And as soon as the doors opened, I saw the next door that we'd walk through—the Exit door. We were about to leave the place that had been our home for four months. The place where our lives had changed. The place that had been full of family and friends. The place where we'd shed tears, held on to hope, looked for joy, had difficult conversations, experienced fear, and persevered through adversity. It was also the place where we'd held on to love, God's promises, and His final say over Paige's life.

Paige had no idea that life existed beyond the walls of the hospital. I continued pushing the stroller toward the exit, and when we got there, my husband reached out again and pushed the button to open the automatic door. When it opened, we pushed Paige through the door.

She was outside. She'd made it out of the hospital.

Outside, the white stretch limo was awaiting our arrival. The limo driver had never met us, but he knew we were the ones he was waiting for. He opened the car doors for us, then stood back as we picked Paige up from the stroller and placed her into her car seat. Once she was inside the limo, I stood back and looked at her. Pink balloons surrounded her, but what stood out to me the most were her big brown eyes. Once again, I was connecting with her through those big brown eyes. This time though, instead of wanting to run, I felt incredibly drawn to her.

I know that no matter what, God has the final say.

It was time for my husband and me to join Paige in the limo. As we drove off, I looked out the window toward the roofline of the hospital. It was getting further and further away. This had been home for four months, but I knew it wasn't home.

Today's the day we're going to our home to live life with Paige.

The Blessing

> *If you know these things, blessed are you if you do them.*
> John 13:17

BEYOND THE WALLS OF the hospital, I hadn't yet lived life with Paige. It was obvious that my current situation now looked a lot different than what I'd imagined or planned. *I have a baby with significant medical challenges. I have a baby who only knows a life full of trauma. I've had doctors who didn't encourage medical intervention. There was no guarantee she would get out of the hospital. I have no way of knowing what life ahead will look like.* What I'd experienced so far was not what I'd thought having a baby was going to be like. Life no longer looked "normal."

As the limo turned into our neighborhood, I saw our home in the distance. As we rolled closer, I saw decorations filling our front yard—pink and white balloons—and signs strategically placed, all welcoming Paige home!

The limo stopped in front of the house. We were home! My husband and I got out of the car, both making our way toward Paige. We couldn't wait for her to see her new home and her new bed. The front door of the house flew open, and people came dashing out. Flashing cameras and rolling camcorders surrounded us. The air was lighthearted and full of chatter.

There was no agenda that day other than to celebrate life. Our immediate family and a few friends each had an opportunity to hold Paige. Everyone could hold her as long as they wanted to without any tubes coming in or out of her. Many people spoke about the four-month journey that had passed. No one talked about Paige's future, what it might look like, because that day none of that really mattered.

After saying goodbye to the last family member, I closed the front door and stood still in the entryway, as my heart experienced a deeper, fuller revelation: *I'm going to be living life with Paige.*

Pondering what this life was going to look like, I decided to walk down the hall toward Paige's bedroom. When I got there, I stood at the doorway and looked in. This time it seemed different. In addition to the painted walls, it now had furniture. I saw a white crib with blue, pink, and yellow bedding against the opposite wall. To my left was a white dresser with a changing table on top. Everything coordinated with the bedding. Next to the white crib sat a gliding rocking chair with a soft blanket on it. Although the room had everything you'd see in a typical nursery, it didn't look like a typical nursery.

Paige's bedroom also had a scattering of medical equipment. There was a machine called a kangaroo pump positioned to the side of her crib. Since she was unable to take a bottle by mouth, we'd use the kangaroo pump to push formula through her G-button during the night. Glancing under the crib, I saw a small black machine, a heart monitor. It was essential to fasten the heart monitor around her at night or any time when she was asleep. The monitor had an alarm that would go off if she needed any medical attention. She also required breathing treatments every four hours, even through the night. The machine for this was in the mix as well as a pulse oximeter to check the oxygen saturation in her blood. We'd camouflaged the equipment as much as possible, but there was no denying or hiding the fact that her room felt much like an abbreviated hospital room.

The instructions they gave us before leaving the hospital were quite extensive. Six different doctors needed to follow Paige: the pediatrician, the neurosurgeon, the cardiologist, the pulmonologist, the neurologist, and the general surgeon. On top of this, we were scheduled to meet with someone from Early Childhood Intervention, and they'd asked us to continue appointments with the Child Study Center. If this weren't enough already, we'd been encouraged to attend the support group that we'd attended once called Our Special Children. My calendar was already filled with follow-up doctor appointments. *How am I going to be able to fit in all of these appointments, take care of Paige, and work full time?*

Insurance was crucial because of Paige's astronomical medical bills and her preexisting conditions. She was already a million-dollar baby, and we'd learned that Lloyd's of London had assisted with her medical bills. My husband was self-employed, so I carried the insurance through my work. Not seeing any other options for me, I'd mentally prepared myself to work at my current job until I retired.

It may have appeared I didn't have a choice, but I did. It's true that I had some unease about knowing how I was going to make it to all of those appointments and work full time. Nor did I know how I was going to do all of the medically necessary things to care for Paige at home. However, I chose to look beyond everything that was in front of me, and instead I chose to celebrate Paige's life and the gift God had given me. Once again, I needed to pull on what was inside me.

I'm not looking back!

Welcome to Holland

Many people know our story, so we've been surrounded by a lot of community. We have people wanting to help us any way they can. Many of our neighbors delivered meals, and my first baby shower was scheduled. It was as if everyone could finally take a deep breath and make a sigh of relief. We were still receiving cards in the mail, and people were constantly speaking encouraging words. I don't remember how I received this poem, but out of all of the things I read during that time, this particular poem spoke to me more than anything else. It's called "Welcome to Holland" by Emily Pearl Kingsley:[1*]

> I am often asked to describe the experience of raising a child with a disability—to try to help people who have not shared that unique experience to understand it, to imagine how it would feel. It's like this.
>
> When you're going to have a baby, it's like planning a fabulous vacation trip—to Italy. You buy a bunch of guidebooks and make your wonderful plans. The Coliseum. The Michelangelo David. The gondolas in Venice. You may learn some handy phrases in Italian. It's all very exciting.
>
> After months of eager anticipation, the day finally arrives. You pack your bags and off you go. Several hours later, the plane lands. The flight attendant comes in and says, "Welcome to Holland."
>
> "*Holland?!?*" you say. "What do you mean Holland? I signed up for Italy! I'm supposed to be in Italy. All my life I've dreamed of going to Italy."
>
> But there's been a change in the flight plan. They've landed in Holland and there you must stay.

---

1 [*]©1987 by Emily Perl Kingsley. All rights reserved. Reprinted by permission of the author.

The important thing is that they haven't taken you to a horrible, disgusting, filthy place, full of pestilence, famine, and disease. It's just a different place.

So you must go out and buy new guidebooks. And you must learn a whole new language. And you will meet a whole new group of people you would never have met.

It's just a *different* place. It's slower-paced than Italy, less flashy than Italy. But after you've been there for a while and you catch your breath, you look around, and you begin to notice that Holland has windmills and Holland has tulips. Holland even has Rembrandts.

But everyone you know is busy coming and going from Italy, and they're all bragging about what a wonderful time they had there. And for the rest of your life, you will say "Yes, that's where I was supposed to go. That's what I had planned."

And the pain of that will never, ever, ever, ever go away because the loss of that dream is a very, very significant loss.

But if you spend your life mourning the fact that you didn't get to Italy, you may never be free to enjoy the very special, the very lovely things about Holland.

This poem spoke directly to me. In a sense, the words describe some of the things I'd gone through. What I'd experienced wasn't what I'd expected. I'd thought that having a baby was going to look different, and I'd planned on things being different—I hadn't planned for this outcome; however, like the poem says, this new place is a beautiful place as well. What stood out to me were the words "if you take the time to notice."

If you take the time to notice.

I didn't dismiss these words. I thought about them and pondered them over and over.

If you take the time to notice.

> The sooner you see the blessing, the sooner you'll receive it! -Sharon Richardson

As I pondered, I began to feel like the poem was speaking to me. *If I focus on what's missing or on what doesn't seem to be here, I might miss out on something beautiful!* I wasn't sure what it meant, but I wanted to give it a try. I wanted to take time to notice. I already knew Paige was a gift God had given me, and I believed God had chosen me out of many for this gift. But I wanted to see more. I wanted to know what my Holland looked like. I wanted to know where to find my tulips.

In my questioning, in my pondering, and in just thinking analytically, I began to realize something else. I began to realize that besides having a gift, I had a blessing. Until now, I'd never given it much thought, but my life had always felt blessed. And now I realized nothing had changed. My life was still blessed, but now my life was blessed with Paige. *She's a blessing that's been added to my life.* Nothing had been taken away from me—instead, something had been added! As a result of my questioning, pondering, and seeking, I was able to have a different perspective about my life. That's when I decided to embrace my blessing.

It was another turning point in my life. My reality was not going to be what I'd thought it would be—yet it was my reality. However, I did have a choice. *What do I do with what's been placed into my hands? Do I embrace it? Or do I complain about it, wishing things were different?*

This new perspective changed me even more. Once I was able to see my situation through another set of lenses, I changed. Paige being a gift had been established, and now I was able to see that Paige was a *blessing* and not a misfortune, hardship, or burden to my life. With this new perspective, I was able to embrace what might have otherwise appeared as a challenge.

As I began walking this out, I began to see that our attitudes are key to receiving. I noticed that when you choose to view your situation differently, your heart begins to change, and as your heart changes, you change. I also experienced the truth that when your heart changes, the way you think changes, the way you feel changes, and the way you interact with others changes. That's when blessings come!

When I started walking this out, I wasn't seeking a blessing, but I knew my thinking had changed. When my perspective changed, it caused the atmosphere around me to change. I began seeing that our attitude changes the atmosphere. Our attitude attracts blessings.

Once again, I found myself walking into situations with my head lifted high, with a positive attitude, and with gratitude in my heart. Now I couldn't wait to tell people about my blessing! How honored I felt knowing God has given her to me. Another key truth was occurring to me too: *If she was going to be born into this world, instead of wondering why me, I should ask the question, why not me?*

I moved to the place of knowing I'd been blessed with a blessing!

I didn't plan it, but people were watching. When they would see me, they saw joy and peace. They'd see something they weren't expecting to see. They were drawn to Paige and me, wanting to be a part of what looked unusual to them. People would offer to help. They wanted to give us gifts. At first, I thought they were just being nice, and they were, but this was different. They could easily have walked away, but instead they were moving toward us.

It was the questions they'd ask that caused me to know they were looking for something more. And what they saw somehow seemed backward. They saw joy in a situation where they didn't understand why there would be joy. They didn't see a burden or any heaviness. They wanted to know more about this.

Over the years, I've been told my life looks different, yet I don't think I'm any different. In fact, I don't see that my life with Paige is any different than that of any other parent of a child with special needs. However, when people have asked about the joy in my life, I've found myself saying over and over again, "The sooner you see the blessing, the sooner you'll receive it!"

I'm here to tell you that no matter what your situation looks like, once you can see it (any situation) as a blessing, things will begin to change. Instead of feeling sorry for yourself, make the decision to move beyond those feelings. In my situation, God had placed a little person into my care. Most assuredly, this wouldn't have been the life or circumstances she would have chosen had she been able to, but it is her reality. Just like everyone else, she has feelings, thoughts, and emotions. She's no different. And just like everyone else, she desires to be loved.

Although I was raised in the church, I hadn't been in church for many years. As soon as I left home, I left church. At the time I thought the only reason someone went to church was to become a good person, and in my mind, I was a good person. However, during that time in my life I needed to see what was inside me and to draw upon those things that made me who I was. I knew I believed in God and was a Christian, but that was about it, yet somehow in the midst of Paige's birth, God was coming back into my life.

God is key because God is love. If you don't bring God into the situation, then I don't believe you'll ever see the blessing. God is a good God. God gives good gifts. If you're a mom or dad, God chose you to be this child's parent. If this baby was going to be born into this world, no matter what, someone needs to take care of them. Why not you? Why not embrace this honoring position for which you've been chosen? Because the sooner you see the blessing, the sooner you'll receive it!

New Beginnings

> *He has made everything beautiful in its time.*
> Ecclesiastes 3:12

INITIALLY I DIDN'T SET out to create an atmosphere of peace. I was just trying to figure out how to get everything done, so I put us on a schedule. Once in place, I was surprised at how quickly I got used to the new routine. Paige was now experiencing order and predictability in her life, yet I knew there was something we hadn't been able to obtain. I knew there was more I could do to help Paige.

How do I bring life to this little body that's in front of me?

As I observed the way she reacted with people, I could see the evidence of fear in her life. Although Paige showed very little emotion or movement, I could see she was easily startled. When I saw her jump or draw back from people, I knew these responses were a result of something going on inside her.

There was a strong feeling in my heart, a kind of knowing or instinct, that Paige needed to recover from trauma. Most of what she'd experienced since entering this world and taking her first breath was trauma.

In the hospital, total strangers had approached her repeatedly to perform medical procedures she had no control over. Over a period of four months, the staff stuck her with needles over and over again, at different hours of the day. She had no concept of why those things happened or why there were so many assaults on her body. I longed for her to be healed from this trauma.

How do I show her that there's more to life than pain and that she doesn't need to fear life or people?

Not only had she experienced trauma, the doctors were saying she had a brain injury. So I began thinking about the brain. *What in the world can heal this brain?* The thought came to me—*peace. She needs peace.* Peace is the opposite of trauma. It made perfect sense to me that the brain needs peace in order to heal. *Paige needs an atmosphere of peace. This is how her brain can heal.* So I set out to give her an atmosphere of peace.

What does peace look like? Not real certain where to start, I spoke calmly to her. I spoke lovingly toward her. I said, "You're precious to me," "You're so beautiful," "You're so special," "Mom loves you very much!" I turned the TV off and played peaceful music. If it felt like peace, I did it. Peace was in our home. It didn't happen overnight, but over time I could see Paige becoming more relaxed and less fearful. She didn't jump when she saw someone.

Since I'd never had a baby before, I wasn't sure how she was supposed to be developing. They'd told us that she was special needs, but what did that really mean? Not knowing all of the different milestones, I began asking around and eventually found a long and very helpful list that spelled out everything for me. The list showed me what Paige should be doing at the different months and years of her life. But as I looked it over, I didn't see anything on it that Paige was doing. Paige was alive, but that was about it. There was very little movement in her body. She had no facial expression, and she was not verbal.

Where do I start?

Smiling

Smiling was the first thing on the list that she wasn't doing. *How do you get someone to smile? How do you teach this? How can I convey that what I'm doing is what I want her to do?* Uncertain how this was going to work, I began opening my mouth, this way and that way. I'd say, "This is a smile," and then I'd smile to show Paige what it looked like. I would smile big and with animation and a great amount of exaggeration—no noise, just big smiles! I did this over and over again, day after day, week after week, month after month, until I finally saw her mouth open! Not only did it open, but I could see that she did it on purpose. I knew that what I'd been doing had registered in her brain.

Paige smiled.

Rolling

One of the next things on the list I did was rolling, because Paige wasn't moving like a normal baby. In fact, her body seemed somewhat stiff. She had what the medical world terms "high tone." I wanted to teach her how to roll and to feel what rolling felt like, so I got down on the floor with her and wrapped my arms around her entire body, and we rolled together. We rolled over and over in one direction, and then we turned right back around and rolled over and over in the other direction.

Once she got used to the feeling of rolling with me, I laid her on the floor and positioned her arms and legs so she could roll by herself. Then without my being connected with her, I helped her roll over and over in one direction. Then I'd reposition her arms and legs and roll her over and over in the other direction. She eventually got the idea that she could move. It's never been easy for her, but to this day, rolling on a mat is one of Paige's favorite things to do.

Talking

Obviously I wanted Paige to talk! Like any parent, I wanted to hear the word "Momma," but I didn't hear any noise from her. I didn't hear a voice. I didn't even hear a cry. We learned that her vocal cords were fine, but there was no outward evidence of this.

One day, a lady from Early Childhood Intervention (ECI) came to our home. ECI was a program recommended to us that helps children with developmental delays, so we gave it a try. I wasn't sure what to expect from the visit.

When the lady arrived, Paige was in the den dressed in one of the many outfits she'd received. She was laying on a lightweight white quilt with pink ruffles, and we both sat on the floor next to her. A bit curious, I found myself gazing at the lady to see what was going to happen next.

She began asking me a lot of questions. "Does she know her name?"

I wanted to say, "She's smiling and she's rolling, but no, she doesn't know her name." I realized I'd been talking to her using cute names, but I hadn't been calling her Paige. This would be the next thing I would teach her.

"I'm going to teach Paige some sign language," the lady said.

Sign language? Her words seemed counter-productive to me. *Why's she planning to do that? It's not what I want—I want Paige to talk. Isn't she going to help Paige talk? I don't want Paige to substitute spoken words with hand gestures.*

I couldn't just sit there—I had to express what I was feeling. She listened to me, and then she encouraged me. So with some hesitation, I decided to go ahead and see what would happen. Some of the first words in sign language that she began teaching Paige were words like Mom, Dad, yes, no, finished, restroom, eat, drink, book, ball, and *more*.

I could see that Paige was interested in what she was doing. She was watching her intently, her eyes engaged. She appeared curious about what she was seeing. I have to admit that there was something about those gestures that registered in Paige. It seemed as if she knew they had meaning.

Over time, Paige began picking up on these words—first one, then another. She was learning a form of communication! Although I still wanted her to talk, I began to warm up to this process. I could see that in learning sign language, other things were happening along with it. Paige was beginning to learn cause and effect, to experience success. She was enjoying a sense of accomplishment, and I could see that this was good.

Eating

Before Paige was born, I'd never known or heard of anyone eating the way she was receiving nourishment, and I wanted her to eat like everyone else. Paige had come home from the hospital with a tube coming from her stomach that was later changed out to a G-button. We hooked this tube up to another set of tubing and then filled the tube with formula. It served its purpose and provided the nourishment she needed, but I was determined she was going to learn how to eat.

The doctors' position was, "We have plenty of time to work on this." But my thoughts were different: *Time is vital. The more time that passes, the more time is lost. Waiting to introduce eating by mouth only means we're missing opportunities.*

So I decided to see for myself and introduced a pacifier. *Every baby likes a pacifier.* However, when I put it in Paige's mouth, it was obvious she didn't have the natural instinct to suck on it. She pushed it out of her mouth. I saw this, but it didn't bother me. *Just because* she pushed the pacifier out of her mouth doesn't mean she can't eat. So, hopeful and expectant, I tried a bottle. And I waited.

It sat there in her mouth, but she didn't know what to do with it. I didn't give up though. I tried it over and over again. Eventually, I saw some of the milk leave the bottle, but she was taking so long to drink even an ounce that it became obvious her mouth didn't have the coordination to take a bottle.

Just because she isn't able to take a bottle doesn't mean she can't eat.

As time passed, I introduced different soft foods, and through trial and error, I began finding a few things that she took interest in and could tolerate. During this season of trying, I discovered she could tolerate soft foods like pudding, yogurt, and Jell-O. I later introduced Vienna sausages and found she liked their flavor. I worked and worked on eating, and Paige began to eat by mouth, though for many years she continued to need her diet supplemented through the G-button. It wasn't until Paige was eighteen that she let me know she didn't want the G-button any longer.

Besides getting used to the new routine and introducing Paige to various developmental milestones, my husband and I walked through the doors of Our Special Children again. This was the same support group we'd attended when Paige was in the hospital, but after this visit I knew, *This isn't for me.*

Just like the other time we'd visited, the room was full of parents with children who had special needs, and they all seemed to be having a difficult time. They shared their stories, but I couldn't relate. I didn't feel like the other parents in the room. In my mind, I didn't have time for this. My focus was spending time with Paige, "my gift, my blessing," and working with her to help her reach her highest potential. We never went back.

In the blink of an eye, it was time to celebrate Paige's first birthday. Family who loved her surrounded her at the birthday gathering we held in our home. Every person there had given us kindness and support during the many ups and downs of the first four months of uncertainty in Paige's life.

I heard no words about the many surgeries Paige had to endure or about all the obstacles we had to overcome. Instead, faces lit up with joy and smiles filled the room.

With full hearts, we all stood around the dining room table and lit the one little candle on the birthday cake, and with everyone's voice chiming in, we sang "Happy Birthday" to Paige.

It was only after the one candle was out that a family member spoke up and said the words that were in all our hearts: "This is undeniably a day to celebrate, because no one knew if Paige would be alive for her first birthday."

It was so true—there were many days, weeks, and months that we didn't know if she would survive. There was never a promise we'd have this day of celebration—one that we'd hoped and longed for. Now we were overwhelmed by the goodness of it all—we had experienced our first year of living life with Paige.

Life and Death

*The thief does not come except to steal, and to kill, and to destroy.
I have come that they may have life and life abundantly.*
John 10:10

THERE WAS NO ESCAPING this surgery. It had been on my mental radar as well as on the monthly calendar for quite some time. But I never could have dreamed that flying to Chicago with Paige would be such a nightmare and an emotional roller coaster.

I'd been back at work for almost a year. After Paige came home from the hospital, I stayed home until I used all my vacation and sick time, which was about two months. Paige continued to be cared for at home instead of daycare, since the instructions were to keep Paige away from germs and known illness for at least the first year.

The surgeon who performed Paige's initial heart surgery had informed us that when she got older, about eighteen months old, she'd need to have an additional surgery to place a valve into her heart. Although we'd had this information, I'd put it out of my mind. But as she approached eighteen months of age, I started having unexplainable feelings.

I can't put a name to those feelings, but the tension was strong, as if a wrestling match were going on inside of me.

What's going on with me? What's this tension I'm feeling? Where are these feelings coming from, and how do I get them to go away?

Not knowing what else to do, I began thinking about my thoughts. As a thought would come to me, I'd ask myself questions about it. *Does this thought bother me?* Yes or no. If the answer was yes, I'd ask myself, *Why am I having this thought, and what does it mean?* Sensing that I was making progress, I did this over and over. Discovering the answer surprised me.

This doesn't make sense. It doesn't make sense, because it's not my idea, yet I have the answer. I know I'm supposed to stay home with Paige after this next surgery. Not only did I know I was supposed to stay home, I knew the length of time—a length that would require me to leave my job, not permanently, but for one year.

I tucked this knowing away in a back pocket initially and told myself, *I don't need to share this with anybody.* But this didn't make the feelings go away. Everywhere I went, there they were. I couldn't get away from them or ignore them, yet I didn't see any possible way for me to take off from work again, much less for one year. I finally began to realize that those feelings were probably not going to go away until I acted on them.

The place where I worked, CSCD, had followed Paige's life closely as a whole, so almost everyone knew Paige would be having this surgery. And they knew I'd be taking off work for her surgery. What they didn't know was how long it would be.

There's no getting around this. I need to let someone know.

Without further delay, I met with the Director of Court Services, but of course I had no idea how she was going to respond. The director was one of my supervisors, but she was also a friend. As I began talking, she listened intently. I opened up and honestly shared my thoughts and intense feelings with her, as well as the fact that they weren't going away.

She didn't say a word. She didn't have to. Until now, what I'd spoken hadn't affected her or anyone else, just me. But I knew my next words were going to impact many people. Taking a deep breath, I let out the words I had to say: "I feel like I'm supposed to take off work for one year to be with Paige."

There. I'd done it. The words were out. I'd spoken them, made the request known.

No one had made a request like this before. Furthermore, a response to this type of request doesn't exist in the current policy and procedure manual. However, they didn't ignore my request. It made its way to the Assistant Director of the department. He got involved immediately, as did the judge I was working for.

I'm not sure what they said in those conversations, but I do know the outcome. They honored my request. And not only did they honor my request, but I had been promoted after Paige's birth, and they held my position as supervisor for one year and didn't fill it! This too had never happened before. I felt overwhelmed with appreciation for their response.

Because I didn't ignore my strong feelings and acted on them, I received something I didn't think was possible. It was actually more than I could have imagined.

Years passed before I knew that what I had experienced is found in the Bible. I was experiencing Ephesians 3:20: "Now to Him who is able to do exceedingly abundantly above all that we ask or think."

I couldn't believe I was going to be able to stay home with Paige for one year! This was incredible news. I felt like hugging everyone's neck. It seemed like everything was falling into place. However, we were about to find out that everything wasn't going to be this easy.

A visit to Paige's cardiologist took us by surprise. We'd always thought we'd be having this surgery at the local children's hospital where Paige had lived for four months. But Paige's cardiologist informed us that the surgeon who performed her initial heart surgery was no longer there.

No longer there?

I couldn't believe what we were hearing. This was the plan all along. After getting over the initial disbelief, I thought, *There has to be another surgeon at the hospital who can do this surgery.* So I asked.

"There's another surgeon on staff," the doctor said, "but that surgeon isn't performing this type of surgery. It will be months before this surgeon will be doing the type of surgery Paige needs."

This decision is getting complicated.

We were in a catch twenty-two. Paige needed to have a surgery that couldn't wait, and there wasn't a surgeon in the area who could perform the surgery she needed. And no one was presenting any other options. Then we had another idea.

"Where did the surgeon go who was here?" *I'm sure she has to be close by.*

"She relocated to the Chicago area."

Chicago? Really? You've got to be kidding. That's not close by. This decision was getting even more complicated.

After many conversations with doctors and family members, as well as phone calls to Chicago, and pondering all of the information within our hearts, we made a decision. What it came down to was relationship. We already had a relationship with this surgeon, and because of this relationship, it only seemed logical to follow her to Chicago. It didn't make sense leaving what was familiar to go there, but following the surgeon did. She was the one who'd performed Paige's first heart surgery, and we felt like she was the one to perform the second one. So we decided to follow this surgeon to Chicago.

Everyone involved began making arrangements for the surgery to take place in Chicago. The surgeon and the medical staff there notified us to plan for a two-week stay. I was just beginning my one year leave of absence from work. Our immediate family struggled a little with this decision. They longed for us to be closer, yet they knew that what we were doing was necessary. The best part was knowing that in two short weeks we'd all be back together. We were ready. With our bags packed, we confidently headed to the airport.

Chicago

Paige looked cuter than ever! We'd made a lot of progress over the past eighteen months, and I'd come to love her personality. Although she was still nonverbal, she now had a lot of facial expressions. She was also sitting up and moving some on the floor. We could interact with her, and she'd respond. Developmental delays were obvious, both physically and mentally, but she was filled with joy and happiness. We'd overcome a lot.

Paige hadn't been on an airplane before, and this was a new experience. She had no idea that this airplane ride was taking her to another state, nor did she know she was about to be back in the hospital again and subjected to yet another surgery. This was not easy to walk out.

I heard our names called over the loudspeaker, and we boarded. Carrying Paige in my arms, I walked onto the airplane where the flight crew greeted us. I felt gratefulness in my heart as I watched Paige interact with them. It was obvious she was enjoying all of the activity and that her level of joy and happiness was increasing.

Due to Paige's current cardiac status, she required oxygen, which was available on the flight because we had made previous arrangements. After finding our seats, one of the flight attendants set everything up for us. Other than watching the safety videos, I'd never seen oxygen used on an airplane before. The tank was located under the seat. The flight attendant said, "Once the airplane takes off, it will become available for use."

As the attendant was leaving, I suddenly became aware of the other people that had boarded the airplane. *Everyone's looking at us. I wonder what they think about this oxygen and Paige.* I felt like we were in the spotlight, and I wasn't sure how to handle it, so I didn't want to look at anyone. I finally peered down the aisle where I began to see the truth.

The truth was, everyone wasn't looking at us. A few people close by couldn't help but notice, but they were very nice, letting me know they were available to help. They could see I was by myself, which was only because my husband had left a day earlier. He drove our car to Chicago so we'd have transportation when we got there. The plan was for all three of us to drive back to Texas.

We're on our way!

Paige enjoyed the sounds and the feeling of the airplane taking off, and as I looked at her, I couldn't help but think how adorable she was. She was making friends with everyone she came into contact with. I had brought a red ball that she kept throwing down the aisle because she didn't know you don't throw red balls down the aisle of an airplane. All she knew was she was having fun. At first I wasn't sure how the people around us or the flight crew were going to react to this, but instead of being annoyed by the bouncing red ball, people kept giving it back to her so she could throw it again. Her actions only brought more kindness and well wishes from everyone around us. We ended up having a very enjoyable time with everyone on the airplane.

Then before I knew it, we'd arrived at our destination. *We're not in Texas anymore!* Everything we'd experienced so far felt more like a new adventure instead of a medical assignment. As we left the airplane, we said goodbye to our new friends. Waiting at the airport was my husband, happy to see us. We were all safe and sound in Chicago. After collecting our luggage, we headed to the hospital.

Driving up, I thought, *It doesn't make sense to bring someone who's so happy and full of joy into the hospital.* It didn't make sense, but it was time. Eighteen months had arrived.

We located the medical staff who were expecting us, and in a matter of minutes we were transitioning from an airplane flight from Texas to a hospital bed in Chicago. They quickly got Paige out of her cute clothes and into a hospital gown. Everyone knew we weren't from Chicago and were very attentive, doing everything possible to welcome us to the area.

Chicago was no longer just an idea—it had become a reality. We'd done all the things necessary to get there. As parents, we wanted to do what was best for Paige. What we didn't realize was that nothing could have prepared us for the days to come.

In late August, the day of Paige's surgery arrived. The staff sedated our joy-filled and happy little girl and took her off to surgery. Just like the day she was born, the doctors told us Paige had a fifty-fifty chance of survival. I must have pushed this information out of my mind to protect my heart because it was as if I were hearing this risk factor for the first time.

After everything she's been through, why would anyone think about putting Paige through such a risky surgery? And why would we do this without the support of family and friends?

It was too late. We couldn't change our minds.

At times, the waiting—the not knowing—felt almost unbearable. I had to keep myself from thinking scary thoughts, imagining what could or could not happen. After twelve long hours of waiting and wondering about the outcome, we finally heard that Paige was in recovery and we could see her.

At these words, I let out a huge sigh of relief. *The fifty-fifty chance of survival must have gone well,* I thought. *The hardest part of not knowing is over.* Everything was going to be fine. But three days later, the doctors noticed an unusual fluid coming from the chest tube, a tube placed during surgery to drain excess blood from around the heart. They decided to pull it out to find out what was going on. Their discovery was the beginning of our nightmare—a nightmare that was still only in its early stages. A nightmare that would come close to breaking all three of us.

As mentioned earlier, Paige had developed hydrocephalus from a bleed inside her brain. This bleed resulted in the inability to absorb spinal fluid, which caused the buildup in her head. A shunt had corrected the problem then. After birth and before Paige ever came home from the hospital, she had undergone multiple surgeries to get a working shunt. This working shunt was necessary to keep her alive, but when the doctors pulled the chest tube out, they discovered that they had cut it during surgery. What they were seeing was spinal fluid and not blood. Although everyone remained calm, a sense of urgency now pervaded the atmosphere.

The hospital immediately called a neurosurgeon to repair her shunt. While I was trying to understand everything going on and remain calm, I could feel my emotions changing from relief to terror. The surgeon could see I was afraid and tried to be kind and reassuring as he explained his plans to place the shunt into Paige's heart.

Her heart? She just had heart surgery. The tubing for the shunt has always been in her abdomen. Why wouldn't it go there again?

They told us that the pressures were too high in her abdomen to receive the tubing there, but since the repair of her heart, this was now an option. *This doesn't seem like a good situation.* I wrestled between hope and fear. But rather than fight it, I chose to see it as a positive solution and be grateful for the option.

The medical staff went into action. Although they had not yet cleared Paige from critical status, they were now prepping her to go back into surgery, this time to repair the shunt. To my relief, she did fine during the surgery, so we all thought everything was back on track. We knew what had happened wasn't good, but no one said a word about it. It was just as if we'd hit a bump in the road and then continued driving.

A few days after the repair of her shunt, I was on my way to see Paige. While walking down the hall toward the ICU, I heard these words over the intercom: "Dr. Respiratory, PEDS-ICU, bed one." Again, I heard, "Dr. Respiratory, PEDS-ICU, bed one."

Paige is in bed one. That's Paige's bed!

I started running as fast as I could—I couldn't get to her fast enough. I ran into the unit and over to her bed, only for a chaplain to lead me away. They wouldn't let me see her—but I had seen. Even as the chaplain was leading me away, I could see all the medical staff working intensely around Paige's bed. She had coded.

"Paige was having a seizure," the chaplain said, "and she stopped breathing. The doctors are trying to revive her so they can put her on a breathing machine."

I knew what I'd seen was a matter of life and death. I'd seen Paige—I'd seen the monitors—and I knew she wasn't breathing. I knew they didn't want me to see it, but I saw the doctors trying to keep her alive. It appeared as if Paige was not going to live.

After I was out in the hallway, I let out a gut-wrenching scream, slid down the side of the wall, and landed in a puddle of tears. I didn't care who saw or heard me because at that moment, nothing mattered. Soon people were surrounding me, trying to comfort me. But I didn't receive it well. I didn't want that comfort. The only thing I wanted was for Paige to live.

The Battle Continues

*For God has not given us a spirit of fear,
but of power and of love and of a sound mind.*
2 Timothy 1:7

I DIDN'T KNOW HOW I was going to survive, for one sword after another was piercing my heart. Not understanding what I'd seen, my husband ran up to comfort me as I sat in a puddle of tears with the chaplain nearby. I could only imagine what was going through his mind. At that moment, one of the doctors walked out of the PEDS-ICU to find us.

"They've intubated Paige—she's stable," he said.

They'd put her on a breathing machine, but a CT scan revealed the shunt wasn't working inside her heart. *I can't believe what I'm hearing. This means another surgery for Paige.*

What we couldn't know at the time was that this next surgery wasn't going to be successful. The surgeon took the tubing from the heart and placed it into the abdomen, but the pressures were still too high for Paige's body to accept it there. Since the heart and the abdomen were the only two places where they could place the shunt, and neither of those options were working, there were no more options. They didn't know what to do. With no answers, the surgeon left the tubing outside of Paige's body. He wanted to wait and see if the pressures would go down in her abdomen. It was a desperate situation, and we were running out of options.

Now we were in a holding pattern. Our two-week stay was turning into three. We were all waiting for the pressures to go down in Paige's abdomen, as well as for her recovery from the initial heart surgery. The medical staff sedated her almost constantly. As I sat beside Paige, I dreamed about the happy little girl throwing a red ball down the aisle of the airplane just days earlier.

By this time, we were wondering why we'd ever left Texas to put Paige through such pain and trauma again. We couldn't understand why this was happening to her. We'd talked with a lot of people and believed that this was what we were supposed to do. And given our options, we believed we'd made the right decision.

Family and friends were calling constantly, checking on Paige, all wanting to know how we were surviving. Everyone was desperate to help, and knowing that we had no family in the area, the nurses and other patients' families were beginning to reach out to us.

Seeking answers and comfort, I found myself looking for the hospital chapel. It was on another level of the hospital. When I walked inside, I thought it looked smaller than I'd expected. No one else was in there, and I sat down on one of the pews and looked around. *It's peaceful in here. I wonder how many other people have been here seeking answers and comfort.* I decided to get down on my knees, and through tears I prayed. I don't remember everything I prayed for, or how long I prayed, but I do know I asked God to keep Paige alive and for us to be able to bring her back home to Texas.

As we entered our second month away from home, the season was changing from summer to fall. The fall weather in Chicago is quite different than the fall weather in Texas. Since my husband and I had only planned for two weeks, we weren't prepared for this change and had to buy warmer clothes. The nurses were now bringing us home-cooked meals, and we'd received meal cards for the cafeteria. Care packages were showing up from family and friends in Texas. In the midst of this unexpected turn of events, we were surrounded by people showing kindness and concern for us, both in Texas and in Chicago.

We couldn't imagine anything else happening to our little girl, but it did. Paige developed a high fever, and consultation immediately began with infectious disease doctors who collected cultures. Tests revealed that Paige had developed numerous infections in her bloodstream from IV lines. The doctors told us she was dying, and they didn't see any possible way for her to overcome what they called "lethal infections inside her body."

I can't believe what we're hearing. She's recovered from the heart surgery, but now she's dying from an infection?

My husband and I burst into heavy, sobbing tears from the deepest places in our hearts. Neither of us could stop crying. Until now, if one of us were having a difficult time, the other would be emotionally strong and able to help the other one. But now that emotional stability no longer existed, and neither of us was emotionally strong enough to handle this news. We knew we needed help, so we called my parents.

I knew I couldn't make the phone call, so my husband made it for us, and I sat there watching as he dialed the number. My mom answered, and my dad was nearby. They knew it was us calling, but we were experiencing so much grief, words couldn't come out. All they heard over the telephone was both of us crying.

My mom was on the first flight out of Texas to Chicago.

We didn't know it at the time, but she'd prepared for this call and already had a ticket ready and waiting. She was a sight for sore eyes, and we both found it comforting to see a familiar face. After seeing us, my mom wanted to see Paige. We prepared my mom the best we could because Paige didn't look the same. In fact, she didn't look anything like she had when she'd arrived.

My mom did see Paige, but of course there wasn't anything she could do to help her. Instead, she focused more on us, speaking words of encouragement to each of us. She ended up staying until we could function again, which was close to a week.

The doctors were treating Paige aggressively with seven antibiotics. We stayed by her bed, talking to her daily, hourly, telling her about the things she was going to do after she came home. What I didn't realize until many years later was that we were speaking life over her with our words. These words were more powerful than I had realized at the time. Paige may have been unresponsive, but she heard them. And I believe those words produced something in the atmosphere, because something changed.

After two weeks, Paige moved. She started moving around, and she woke up.

The doctors couldn't believe that she'd survived such a lethal infection, and they knew they'd witnessed a miracle. We didn't think about it being God at the time, but I remember saying to the doctors, "There's one thing that medicine can't cure—it's called *love*!" Paige was awake after being unresponsive for two weeks, but she was still in the hospital, and she didn't have a working shunt. We already knew we needed to get her out of this hospital. It was time to leave and get her back to Texas.

We'd been asking around for a while to see what it would take to get Paige back home. The medical staff, our insurance carrier, and family members worked fervently on a plan to get us home—and with everyone's help, it happened!

The Battle Continues

Texas

The day came when Paige and I found ourselves on a very small airplane headed back to Texas. This wasn't your typical airplane, but obviously a medical flight, because medical equipment filled the plane. In fact, it resembled the inside of an ambulance. Only four of us flew on this plane: the pilot, a nurse, Paige, and me. Paige was on a bed dressed in a hospital gown. She had what is known as an external drain, a tube coming out of her head to drain the spinal fluid from her brain. She still needed another surgery, which she would receive back in Texas. Although we knew she'd have to undergo this surgery, we felt hopeful we were moving in the right direction.

I don't remember much about the actual flight, other than getting on the airplane and then landing at a small airport. Once the plane landed, an ambulance transported Paige and me to our local children's hospital. To my surprise, as I stepped out of the ambulance, I saw my brother Eric standing there waiting for us. I couldn't believe he was there to greet us, and tears began to rise up from inside and then to flow—tears of gratefulness and tears of joy.

Feeling loved! We were home!

We'd returned to a hospital familiar to us, to a home to go to, and to family and friends who would surround us, yet Paige was in need of another miracle. While the rest of the family waited for us in the waiting room, the hospital staff took Paige directly from the ambulance to the Intensive Care Unit.

Being surrounded by our family helped our overall sense of well-being. When my brother went into the ICU to see Paige though, he had a troubling experience he shared with all of us afterward.

"They have a Dixie cup sitting on top of Paige's head with a needle coming out of it," he said. "And I heard the doctors say, 'We're making her comfortable. We're doing this for the family.'"

As I heard this, a flood of memories came rushing in. *We're back in this place that hasn't given us hope or encouragement, and they're basically saying they don't expect her to live or to leave the hospital. But I don't agree! God has the final say here. The doctors don't know.* However, I couldn't ignore the fact that we had a huge mountain in front of us.

While we were all sitting there, one of the doctors came out to talk with us. He basically told us what my brother had heard.

"They're making her comfortable," he said.

Tears and silence filled the room.

We didn't bring her all the way back to Texas to hear this news. We're going to give Paige every possible chance of survival, God has the final say over her life. Paige is going to have the surgery she needs.

The neurosurgeon in Texas placed the shunt back into Paige's body, and she was able to come home, but if I hadn't known that Paige was my daughter, I might not have recognized her. She sure didn't look like the same little girl I'd known just two months earlier, because her skin was red and rough from all of the medications she'd received in Chicago, and her body was extremely swollen all over. She had numerous cuts, scabs, and scars from the top of her head to the soles of her feet, and she had no hair on her head. She couldn't sit up anymore, and her body was listless. Her smile was gone.

The Power of Words

As we left the hospital, I started hearing words in my head, the words spoken by the surgeon after he did the surgery, and I couldn't get them out of my mind. They consumed my thoughts.

They were, "Time will tell."

Many people don't realize how much power is in their words. Words we hear can have a direct impact on our future thoughts. Whether he meant it or not, those words meant something to me.

When I thought about these words, they didn't feel hopeful—instead they caused me to doubt. They didn't sound positive or encouraging. They actually brought fearful thoughts. Instead of bringing joy, peace, and comfort, those three words caused me to question.

What's the future going to look like with Paige? How many days are we going to have with her?

Death and life are in the power of the tongue. (Prov. 18:21)

I didn't know this Scripture then, but I did know that these words affected my thoughts. These words were not producing life. There was definitely power in these words.

I didn't have a name for it at the time, but I later realized that I had experienced trauma. These words were not helpful in me overcoming this. This time after coming home from the hospital, I found myself on the couch curled up in a fetal position holding Paige in my arms. My heart was broken. As I lay there, I prayed for her to live and for her joy to return.

I wasn't quite sure how to move forward. My mind raced with various thoughts. I didn't know what life looked like besides holding onto Paige, almost clinging to her. According to those words, I didn't know how much time I'd have with her. And I didn't know how to get those words or those thoughts out of my mind.

Then something happened.

I had this feeling that I was supposed to find my Bible. I'd had a Bible for many years, but I wasn't familiar with it. I knew some of the basics, like there is an Old and New Testament. I knew where to find some of the books in the Bible, but I'd never read them. Other than being moved to go get my Bible, I wasn't sure what I was doing. Not knowing where to look, I began flipping through some of the pages. And that's when I came across a verse that stood out. When I read the words, it was like they jumped off the page. So I read them again: "Trust in the Lord with all of your heart and lean not on your own understanding" (Prov. 3:5).

Those words spoke to me. *I definitely have no understanding. I have no understanding or explanation for why or what we just went through. I definitely don't know what tomorrow is going to bring. There are a lot of things I don't know.* There was something about this verse that got my attention and caused me to keep looking at it. I kept reading it over and over again.

As I continued reading, something was happening inside of me. I began thinking, *I need to stop feeling sorry for myself. I need to look beyond my own feelings.* Then my thoughts turned into questions: *How can I make life better for Paige?* And it came to me: *I'm going to do what this verse says and trust God, even though I don't understand.*

I didn't realize it at the time, but this verse was speaking life to me. Just like the surgeon's words, these words had meaning too. However, these words had a positive effect on me—they were encouraging and gave me hope. There was no fear in these words. I felt strengthened when I thought about trusting God, even though I didn't understand what that meant or looked like. Unlike the words the surgeon spoke, these words were life-giving!

When I made the decision to look beyond myself, I could see that although Paige's heart had been medically repaired, it was very broken. *She's experienced so much trauma.* Although I knew it was still Paige, she was not the same person. She wasn't the same Paige who'd thrown a red ball on the airplane, surrounded by people laughing and enjoying her cuteness. Now when I looked at her, she had no joy. There was no evidence of happiness. No zest for life. No emotion. None.

I began to have other thoughts, *She's the innocent one here. She didn't ask for this. She's the one who has to overcome a life with possible disabilities. How can I help her?* That's when I found myself doing the only thing I knew to do—to pour my love into her, every which way I knew how.

Initially I found myself thanking God for Paige. I would go into her bedroom each day to see how she was doing, basically to see if she was still alive. Then I would thank God for another day with Paige. Each day I was filled with gratitude that she still had breath in her body. Thanking God daily and out loud became a routine for many years.

"Thank You, God, for another day with Paige!"

"Thank You, God, for another day with Paige!"

"Thank You, God, that Paige woke up."

"Today is a good day because Paige woke up!"

Even today, Paige will periodically say, "Paige woke up!"

And I will respond, "Yes, she did. Today is a good day because Paige woke up."

It didn't take me long before I realized I was learning at a much younger age what's important in life. When you're faced with a life and death situation, it puts your entire life in perspective. Things that once seemed important begin to have little meaning. I discovered that another day with Paige was what was most important. Life may be full of trials, but when you wake up each morning and the loved ones around you wake up too, it's going to be a good day.

Besides thanking God for Paige, I would hold her. I no longer clung to her from a place of fear, because that old place of fear in my heart was no longer the focus. It no longer had my attention. When I held Paige, I'd wrap my arms all around her little body and hug her tight. These were not quick hugs but intentional hugs where I purposed in my heart to connect with her. Somehow I was hoping that these hugs would convey how much I loved her. Although she didn't respond or reciprocate, I hugged her when she woke up, when

How Deep Is Your Love?

she went to bed, and throughout the day. My heart was overwhelmed with gratefulness that I was living life with Paige.

The New Normal

None of these things move me; nor do I count my life dear to myself, so that I may finish my race with joy.
Acts 20:24

PAIGE AND I WERE both learning to trust again. It wasn't that we didn't want to trust, but unexpected events and unexplained outcomes had filled our lives.

I wanted to know why Paige was still on oxygen. During the months leading up to the heart surgery, she'd begun requiring it, but it was always my understanding that her need for it was only an indicator that it was time for her to have the surgery. They'd assured us that once the surgery was completed, she wouldn't need it anymore.

No one could give us an explanation why she still needed it, leaving me somewhat baffled and puzzled. *Why in the world did we put her through so much? Outwardly, she looks worse. We went through all of this, and it doesn't look like there's any improvement.*

Although no one had an answer, one thing was certain. Paige needed to be on oxygen full time. She couldn't go anywhere without it.

I now had another choice, another opportunity to move beyond my current set of circumstances. There may not have been an explanation, but what I did know was that being on oxygen full time was not going to keep us confined. I decided to take off what felt like limitations on us. I decided that Paige and I were going to go out—we were going to celebrate life outside the walls of the house.

I picked Paige up, oxygen in tow, and placed her into the stroller. She wasn't able to sit up anymore, so I stacked pillows behind her back, piling them until she could sit upright. I wanted her to be able to see what was going on around her. I then placed the oxygen tank in the stroller, and we walked through the garage and down the driveway.

Sunshine met our faces, and we breathed in the fresh air. Everything felt bright and the world at ease. *This is where we're supposed to be. It feels right.* As we continued walking through the neighborhood, some of the neighbors greeted us, wanting to visit. Many of them had made meals for our family right after Paige was born. They'd been following her life.

Walking around the neighborhood was just the beginning. I began taking Paige everywhere. If she wasn't in her stroller, I had her in one arm, with my other hand holding onto the oxygen tank rolling beside us. To others it may have looked like our life had some restrictions. Maybe so, but I didn't allow them to limit us. We were living life and living it fully. I didn't do this for anyone except for Paige, but other people were watching.

Paige's body was still red and swollen. She had bristles of hair on her head, and her eyes were open, but she showed no visible emotion. If I'd allowed it, I could have reacted to the people watching by feeling awkward and uncomfortable, but I chose not to let any of the looks bother me. Instead, I held my head high, proud of my daughter, knowing she was perfect and that no matter what she looked like, she was beautiful.

When I saw people looking our way with curiosity, I would stop and strike up a conversation instead of continuing on our way. I would introduce Paige and share how special she is. The natural tendency was to ask, "What's wrong with her?" But since I didn't see anything wrong with her, I'd reply, "Nothing's wrong with her. She just needs oxygen to help her feel better." Most of the time this would satisfy their curiosity.

I soon became aware of how many people were watching. But this time I began to realize that the curiosity wasn't necessarily about Paige. Rather, they were watching how I was interacting with her. I began to understand I was witnessing to people through my actions. People would say to me, "You make it look so easy." Although those words were nice to hear, I usually thought, *This is what anyone would do, right? I'm just choosing to live life.*

I don't remember how long it took, but Paige did start changing. Her skin color improved, the swelling in her body went away, and the hair on her head grew back. I've always believed that medical doctors and surgeons have a part in healing the body physically, but I was beginning to see that Paige was receiving additional healing from her environment.

More important than Paige's outward appearance was the change taking place in her heart. Her heart had healed physically after surgery, but I could see it was now repairing emotionally. Now when I looked at her, I'd think, *Her heart's healing. The evidence of trauma is leaving her body. She's not afraid like she used to be.*

The day when I saw Paige smile again only confirmed the inward changes that I knew were happening inside her. No words can begin to convey what it was like for me to see her smile again. When I saw her precious face light up, I knew in that moment *she's back. Like me, she's trusting again.*

The Fundraiser

My employer, CSCD, as a whole faithfully stood by our family. Many were in contact with us on a regular basis, and everyone knew what had happened in Chicago. They celebrated Paige's life and our return to Texas. What I didn't know was they had also organized a fundraiser to raise money for us.

I received a copy of the letter that had gone out to all of the employees regarding this fundraiser. The letter came from the Assistant Director, the same person who was so instrumental in granting my leave of absence. It revealed their desire to help our family through financial provision. As I read it, the words stirred my heart deeply. *I can't believe people want to do this for us.* I became overwhelmed with gratitude and tears began to flow. Here are some of his words from the letter:

> In the near future you'll be hearing about a very tough and brave family. They're special to us in the department because they are part of us.
>
> Early last year, Sharon gave birth to a beautiful baby girl. Paige Richardson came into this world prematurely and with profound medical problems, including a severe heart defect.
>
> Her early survival was in doubt. But the doctors didn't realize something at the time; Paige is a fighter and she is determined to live.
>
> Now, nineteen months later, after nine major surgeries, she's still fighting. Sharon has taken a leave of absence to be with Paige as she struggles toward life as a healthy child.
>
> A group of fellow CSCD employees are going to be organizing a major fund-raising activity on Paige's behalf. As these activities are planned and conducted, we hope that many of you will come forward to volunteer some time and effort.

> I know that all of us in the department will reach out to the Richardson family in whatever ways possible during the upcoming months.
>
> Please think of this little fighter who wants so badly to live and thrive. What a rare opportunity we have to help part of our family.

My friends and coworkers were rallying together in support of our family. Not only was this letter sent throughout the department, but I was asked to provide a family photo to put on a flyer. They posted flyers around the county, notifying people of the opportunity to give a financial contribution to our family.

At random times, complete strangers walked up to me to tell me they recognized me from a photo they'd seen, maybe in an office or on an elevator. Although I knew all of this was going on, the first time someone came up to me, it felt very surreal.

This must be someone else's life, not mine!

I couldn't believe this was our family they were talking about. It was obvious the people I worked with loved our family. They loved Paige. They went above and beyond to help our family, which showed us how deeply they cared for us.

The department's fundraiser was very successful. At Christmastime, they presented us with a check that helped cover many of our expenses while I was still off from work. However, time continued to pass, and my leave of absence was about to end. The day I was scheduled to return to work was getting closer and closer.

Different people started asking me, "Are you returning to work or have you changed your mind?" I hadn't changed my mind. We still needed the insurance. I didn't have a choice in this decision; I needed to go back.

My response was always, "Yes, I'm coming back."

Will Anyone Say "Yes"?

It was obvious going back to work meant I wouldn't be able to stay home with Paige. What wasn't obvious was who was going to take care of her. Just like during her first year, the doctors discouraged public daycare. We understood this, the difference this time was that Paige was on oxygen full time.

I began asking around and discovered a list of providers licensed through the state who take care of children in their homes. *This is perfect, just what I've been looking for.*

Once I had this list, I looked at all the names and imagined what these people looked like, how they took care of their homes, and the children they watched. *Out of all of the people listed,* I wondered, *who's the one that's going to take care of Paige?* I looked at the various addresses and the different areas of town, and I marked the ones that seemed to stand out. I was ready to make the first call.

It didn't take me long to discover that other people didn't feel the same way that I did about taking care of Paige. Just because I thought Paige was easy to care for didn't mean others felt the same way. My telephone calls went a little like this:

"Hi! This is Sharon Richardson. I found your name on a list of licensed caregivers." After the introductions, I began telling them about Paige.

"I have a daughter who's two and a half years old, and her name is Paige. She is special needs." Then I'd wait to see what kind of response I'd get. If they were okay with this, then I'd share the next thing.

"She's physically and mentally challenged."

Again, I'd wait for a response. At this point, some people graciously declined. Others would ask me to share more about the special needs, so I'd give more explanation. If they were still on the telephone after I shared, I felt hopeful.

Throughout the conversation, I always knew I had one more thing to share, and I'd think, *If they're okay with this next thing, then I have a potential sitter!* It was hard getting the words out though, and I would've preferred to stall and take more time. *Maybe if I speak what I have to say fast enough, they'll say yes before they know what they're saying yes to.*

I'd practically close my eyes, shake my head, and take in a deep breath. Then I'd say, "She's on oxygen full time!" After letting out a breath, I'd wait. Most of the time there was an awkward silence, and I knew by the silence what the answer was going to be.

I purposed in my heart that I wasn't going to let those responses affect me though, so I'd go to the next number on the list. However, one by one, over and over again, the answer was, "I'm sorry, but I'm not going to be able to help you." I called everyone on this list—well over one hundred telephone calls; I'm not exaggerating here—which meant I had to hear the words, "I can't help you" over one hundred times. I hadn't expected this. In fact, I'd never given it any thought because I'd always assumed someone would be there to help. But eventually the reality faced me that I didn't have anyone to take care of Paige—not one person.

A bit of desperation started setting in. *What am I going to do?* My mind raced, grasping for possible solutions. *I have an idea! I'm going to call the church!* The church I had in mind was near our home. We didn't attend there, but they knew who we were from our extended family. There was a daycare at this church.

I realized that going in this direction meant Paige wouldn't be in someone's home. *It's a daycare, but not a public daycare, right?* I really didn't know what was right, but I did think it was a good idea, so I called and explained to the man on the other end of the line what I was up against and asked him if the church could help.

His first response was, "I'm not sure."

What? He's not sure? I couldn't believe what I was hearing. It began to feel like another door was about to shut. The next words I spoke came from a place of desperation. I said, "If the church can't help me, how can I expect anyone else to?"

Yes, those words did come out of my mouth. And yes, there was silence on the other end of the line. In fact, both ends were silent.

But then he spoke. "Let me see what I can do."

As it turned out, the church did agree to care for Paige for a short period of time. I felt optimistic as the weight lifted off my shoulders.

Since I still had some time before I had to return to work, I posted a photo of Paige on the church's bulletin board asking for help. It felt much like placing an ad. I wasn't really expecting anything to come of it, but nevertheless, my phone rang. It was Lisa. I didn't know Lisa. I'd never met Lisa before, but she'd seen Paige's picture on the bulletin board. Until now, no one had seen Paige; they'd just heard about her through telephone calls. Now this person Lisa had actually seen Paige.

Anyone looking at the photo would have known Paige was on oxygen, so there was nothing left for me to share. Lisa already knew, and the next words that came out of Lisa's mouth were the sweetest.

"I have a daughter about the same age and thought maybe I can help out some way."

I couldn't believe what I was hearing. Instead of "I can't help you," someone was actually saying they wanted to help! I had just received a miracle telephone call! I had someone to help me with Paige!

The day arrived when my one-year leave of absence came to an end. When I'd made the initial request, I had never dreamed of such a nightmare, of the emotional roller coaster ahead. Paige was now two and a half years old, and she'd been through a lot. We'd all been through a lot—more than the words on these pages can truly convey. But Paige was alive, she was healing, and life was good. For the first time, life felt normal. It may not have looked normal to others, but it was our normal, and life with Paige was good.

Fullness of Life

*You will show me the path of life;
In Your presence is fullness of joy;
At Your right hand are pleasures for evermore.*
Psalm 16:11

LIFE WAS SO NORMAL that we actually rejoiced when Paige experienced a normal childhood disease. Among the gifts she received on her third birthday was chickenpox. In one way, this health event was more normal than anything else we'd experienced so far in her life. Once we realized what was going on in her, we actually thought, *We're finally experiencing something we could have anticipated!*

Turning three also meant it was time to go to school. Over those first few years, I worked with Paige at home doing many things. Besides smiling, rolling, sitting, talking, and eating, I introduced blocks, books, textures, puzzles, beads, and games, among other things, yet it was obvious she wasn't developing like other children. She wasn't talking like a three-year-old. She wasn't walking like a three-year-old. There were many things she wasn't doing. Because of these obvious developmental delays, both physical and mental, we'd enrolled her in the Special Education program in our school district.

Anticipation filled the first day of school as the big yellow bus pulled up in front of our house. Paige and I saw the bus together from our kitchen window.

"Paige," I exclaimed in delight. "The bus is here! The bus is here! You get to ride the bus today!"

She hadn't ridden a bus before, and I longed in my heart for an exciting experience for her. I began gathering what I'd planned for Paige to take to school. Then I picked her up and carried her out to the bus, with an oxygen tank in tow. The bus driver greeted Paige and me as we got onto the bus.

Once inside, I looked around to find the best seat and found the one behind the bus driver open. *This looks like a good place for her to sit. She'll be close to the bus driver and can see out of the front window.* After making sure she was properly secured, I gave Paige a hug and a kiss and began walking off the bus. Then I turned back to take another look at her. She was looking at me with those big brown eyes. I'm pretty sure she had no idea where she was going. She hadn't been to school before, nor did she have any concept of its meaning. As I looked at her, a number of thoughts went through my head.

I can't believe she's going to school.
She looks out of place sitting on this big bus.
She's only three years old.

A lump began to form in my throat. *I need to keep moving. She's going to be fine. This is going to be a great day!*

Paige came to love the bus, and the bus ride soon became a highlight of her day. It came to our home every morning and every afternoon, year after year, for nineteen years. Besides the big yellow bus, there were many other experiences during those school years that were meaningful to her. A few things I found helpful during those years of raising a child with special needs were music, communication, and development.

Music

From the time Paige was born until now, she'd been exposed to music. The kind of music Paige listens to has changed, but the effect of music on her has not.

Paige's first exposure to music occurred only days after she was born. She received a red wind-up music box that had Big Bird from *Sesame Street* on the front. We placed the music box inside her incubator and played it over and over again. The only song it played was simple and repetitive, yet soothing, releasing a sense of calmness. We still have the music box. It runs a lot slower now but still plays. We played it so much during the four months Paige was in the ICU that we no longer need to wind it up to hear the music playing. I can just look at it and hear the music in my head.

I don't remember Paige's formal introduction to the singing dinosaur, but I vividly remember when I first laid eyes on him. It was in Chicago, and Paige was in critical condition. I was standing beside her bed, praying for another miracle in her body, and as I stood there, I looked around the room. It was full of other toddlers who had also undergone heart surgeries. Over time, I'd watched many of these other children get better and leave the critical care unit, but Paige remained there. On this particular day, I was observing a young boy who was watching a singing purple dinosaur on the television monitor above his bed.

I began feeling a little annoyed by this dinosaur—how happy it was and how happy this young boy was as he watched it sing. The little boy appeared healthy and without a care in the world, and I realized I'd give anything to have some of that in our lives. Little did I know this singing dinosaur who annoyed me would become a part of our family for life.

Sometime after we returned to Texas, Paige spotted this singing dinosaur. When I saw him, I knew I'd seen him before. *Oh yes, I* remember. *This is the singing dinosaur I saw in Chicago. I'm not sure if I like him or not. This is the dinosaur who seems so happy.* His name was Barney.

As I watched Paige, I could see she liked him. She was happy, just like the boy I'd observed in Chicago. There was something about the music, the singing, the upbeat songs, and how the songs related to life that she enjoyed. It didn't take me long to change my mind about this singing dinosaur. Somehow, he made me happy too.

One of Barney's songs that Paige especially enjoys is the "I Love You" song. Over the years, we've sung the words of this song together. "I love you. You love me. We're a happy family, with a great big hug [this is where we hug], and a kiss from me to you [this is where we give kisses]. Won't you say you love me too?" This is when we say, "I love you."

To this day, when we hear Barney begin to sing the "I Love You" song, Paige will say, "It's on! It's on!" This is my cue to run to her so we can sing together and give each other hugs and kisses.

It became evident that music speaks to Paige on a different level, so my husband and I placed her in music therapy. During music therapy, different concepts and ideas, like counting, learning animal names, and so on, came alive when put to music. There's something about music that helps Paige understand. Each time she became involved in another aspect of music, it became more apparent that it would be a big part of her life.

In church, Paige experienced traditional hymnal music. But when she was in her teens, she encountered more nontraditional, catchy, upbeat music, and where we noticed a greater change in her countenance. This music causes her to dance, to move her body and smile with great delight! Once this connection was made, her music inventory radically changed. One of her early favorites was the song "Blessed Be Your Name" by Matt Redman. She played this song over and over and over again. Another song near and dear to her heart during this season was "How Great Is Our God" by Chris Tomlin. Again, something about the beat and the words of this song bring her joy and cause her to dance!

One day when Paige was listening to her music, I found her crying. I wasn't sure what was going on because I hadn't seen her like this before. Her music was playing, so I listened closer to hear what she was listening to. I heard Kari Jobe singing the song "You Are Good" by Gateway Worship.

This song is affecting Paige.

"What's happening?" I asked her.

She indicated she didn't know.

"Are you happy or sad?"

"Happy," she said.

When I heard this reply, I knew—I knew in my heart that the Holy Spirit was moving on her and this song was healing some deep places in her heart. Somehow this song was reaching feelings and emotions that Paige wasn't able to express verbally.

Paige praises God. When we're in any worship setting, whether corporate, in the car, or in our living room, when there's a familiar song playing or the music has a catchy beat, it's almost like a light switch turns on—she wakes up! She comes alive! She can't stop herself from lifting up her arms in praise. She'll begin to bounce up and down and swing her body back and forth. Many people have observed her doing this and commented on how watching Paige worship and praise God ministers to them.

Let everything that has breath praise the Lord. (Ps. 150:6)

It's my belief that music has helped enormously to bring Paige into more fullness of life. Given the right music choices, the words she hears and the various beats and rhythms continue to have a positive influence on her. It's fun to see how music can change someone's countenance and mood, just like that!

> While I live, I will praise the Lord;
> I will sing praises to my God, while I have my being. (Ps. 146:2)

Communication

I believe communication is extremely important—in fact, it's key. It's always been my aspiration to understand what Paige is saying, and I've placed a high priority on it. As mentioned earlier, Paige was introduced to sign language when she was only a few months old. Although I initially resisted, sign language ended up being more helpful than I'd first expected. I began to see that through signing, Paige's hands could do something her mouth wasn't able to do yet.

It didn't take long for Paige to understand that moving her hands a certain way had an effect on her environment. She discovered that when she touches all of her fingers together on each hand in the shape of an O and taps the tips of her fingers together, it means something. It means she's signing the word more, and this word has meaning. She likes this. *More* is a fun word. *More* means she gets to keep doing something she likes! The word more has turned into a signature word for Paige, and in fact in Paige's life, the word more means "absolute delight"!

Paige's signing was very basic, yet it was helpful. But the day came when she started to speak! What was inside of her began coming out. I knew they were words, though they didn't have any meaning to me. Although I had no idea what she was saying, I did know she was trying to communicate something to me.

As I studied her, I could see she was developing her own language. She was communicating! I soon recognized I needed to learn what she was saying. I didn't want to lose out—those words were a way to connect with her, to understand her, to know her better. *This is vital. Paige needs to know that what's coming out of her mouth has purpose and meaning, and the potential to change her world.*

My training began. When words came out of her mouth, I wouldn't leave her side until I was certain we'd communicated. It's been a lot like charades at times, and often I've wondered, *Is this the time I'm not going to be able to understand her?* I purposed in my heart I wasn't going to leave her hanging. It hasn't always been easy, but every time it happened, I never left her side until I was able to understand.

I've found it helpful, if I'm able, to determine the context in which she's communicating—whether about family, school, home, or the past, present, or future.

In our early days when I was having a difficult time understanding, I would pick Paige up and carry her around the house, asking her if she could show me.

One day she was asking for something in the kitchen. What I heard her saying was, "Want tack. Want tack." But her words didn't make sense to me. So I picked Paige up and asked her, "Can you show me? Can you point to it?" She understood what I was saying and pointed to a cabinet. I carried her over to the cabinet and opened the doors. There were sacks inside, so I pointed to them.

"Sacks?"

She said, "Yes, tack."

Of course, tack! It's so obvious! Obvious to Paige. And obvious that I was the one learning. The best thing about that moment is that we communicated!

I also realized that Paige thinks out of the box. Many times the method she uses to communicate looks different, yet it reveals creative thinking. For instance, once Paige said to me in her language, "Go ahead." I understood the word go but not the word *ahead*. She knows when I'm not understanding, which in itself is helpful. So once she realized I wasn't getting it, she put her hand on her head. This caused me to press in and think because I could see she had her hand on her head.

"Go head?" I said.

She nodded yes.

Once I received the yes, I knew *she* had communicated, and now it was time for *me* to make sense of it. I pondered what she was saying until it clicked for me.

Oh! I get it! "Go ahead?"

Once again she affirmed it, and we celebrated the fact that she communicated and I understood.

Here's one more example of this creative thinking. Paige was trying to communicate the word *next*. I wasn't getting it. Once again, she knew I wasn't understanding her, so she started pointing to her neck.

I said, "Neck?"

She said, "No." But she didn't take her hand off her neck; she kept pointing to it.

She knows what she's talking about here—it's me who's not understanding. So I pondered what she was doing until I had an *aha* moment. Once I was able to connect the dots, I said, "Next?"

She said, "Yes!"

And we celebrated!

I've always celebrated communication with Paige. Even today as she continues to put longer sentences together, conveying new concepts and using bigger words, we celebrate. She currently uses words like "absolutely" (thank you, Aunt Lucy) and "dramatic." She knows they carry some weight, and she has fun using them. Sometimes I affectionately refer to her language as "the Paige language." But who's to say that her language is not the perfect language?

I have a strong belief in my heart that Paige's success in communication has had a direct effect on her happiness. She has a voice, and she's been heard. I also believe that her ability to have a way to communicate has lessened the potential for her to become angry or frustrated. This process requires patience, determination, and dedication, but the reward of a happy child, one without frustration, is priceless.

Developing

I'm a developer. I have a strong belief that everyone has potential and everyone can grow. I've always chosen to take labels and limitations off people. As a result of this natural tendency, I've encouraged Paige to do things others may not have thought possible.

There's something in each of us that feels good after we've been able to accomplish a task—even more so when it wasn't easy to do. It creates a sense of satisfaction, making us feel good about ourselves. I believe these feelings of accomplishment cause us to be willing to try again.

Since I tend to see things this way, I've allowed Paige to do everything she can easily do. In addition, I've stretched her by encouraging her to do more difficult things—things she and others may think are impossible. None of this has ever been about "fixing" her because that would mean it's more about me than about her.

Paige is small and petite, looks younger than she is, and moves between a walker and a wheelchair. Although she's able to walk with a walker, she's not very fast. Most everything she does is at a slower pace. Many people want to help her, which is kind; however, too much of this doesn't give her opportunities to experience success, or even failure.

My desire is to give her the time she needs so she's able to do the things she can do easily. She likes it when she does things by herself. She now tells me, "Do it by myself." Through these opportunities, she's been able to experience the feeling of success, and the sense of her own identity and self-worth.

I've also given Paige opportunities to be stretched. In fact, I look for them. When I see something she hasn't tried or experienced, I visualize in my head what it might look like for her to do it. If I think she's capable, we try it. If it doesn't look like it's going to work, we stop. Most times we end up accomplishing something new—and it's exciting!

I've never ignored or dismissed something that may be hard. When she's trying something new, I acknowledge the fact that what's in front of her is hard. I also encourage her by saying things like, "I know this is hard, but I know how strong you are. I believe you can do it." Or I might say, "You're so smart. I'm so proud of you for trying." When Paige receives this type of encouragement, she's willing to try. I'll stand by her side, watch her, and help if needed, but most of the time she finds out for herself that she's capable of doing the thing I put in front of her—that "thing" she didn't think was possible.

Paige has experienced many new things in her life with success, things she'd never known. (I'll share more later.) In the process, I've never tried to "fix" her. The way I see it, fixing is not developing. "Fixing" comes from a place of frustration inside oneself, causing you to look at the person in front of you and to see something broken. For me, developing is looking at the person in front of you and seeing the beauty inside of them. It's in this acceptance that the beauty comes forth.

> I am fearfully and wonderfully made;
> Marvelous are your works. (Ps. 139:14)

I've always set out to help Paige reach her fullest potential, but I've desired this for her, not for me. I encourage everyone to find something you know your loved one can do and to celebrate that! Then find something you think they can't do and give it a try! You may never know what they're capable of doing if you don't try. We've tried many new and wonderful things as we've lived life with Paige.

God's Idea, Not Mine

*There are many plans in a man's heart,
Nevertheless the Lord's counsel—that will stand.*
Proverbs 19:21

I WORKED EIGHT MORE YEARS, and then God brought me home from work. It was God who did it because I had no intention of leaving my job. We'd come a long way and made a lot of progress. Paige was ten years old. She'd been off of oxygen full time since she was four years old, and now she was in fifth grade. After school, the bus took Paige to a licensed childcare provider in their home. I was in a regular routine and quite comfortable, and I had no plans to make any changes. The decision to work until I could retire was still the plan. Or so I thought.

During this season, my husband was in Bible Study Fellowship (BSF), a weekly Bible study. It may be different now, but at that time, if you wanted to complete the entire study, it would take seven years.

When a friend invited him to go, I found myself feeling a little jealous. I'd heard about BSF before, so I knew what that invitation meant. We were going to church now and had been attending since Paige was two or three years old, but I wanted to go to BSF. I wanted to learn more about the Bible, yet I couldn't see how I could possibly fit it into my schedule.

I watched him read the Bible and do the homework. It became obvious that this study was a commitment, and I could see that he was committed. I watched him study week in and week out, the time commitment only confirming what I already knew—there was no way I could fit this into my schedule. Instead of feeling jealous though, I chose to change those feelings into happiness for him. My heart became full of joy that he was able to attend.

It wasn't long after my husband began BSF that he brought up the idea of my coming home from work. I was in the kitchen making dinner one evening when he mentioned it, but I dismissed his words. Although he had a job now where he could carry the insurance, I still thought it would never be a possibility. So even though I heard him, I wasn't sure he was really serious. It wasn't until he called me at work that I realized how serious he was.

We usually don't call each other at work during the day, which is why I knew this call was important. We said our hellos, and then he didn't say a word. I knew he was trying to say something, so I waited. Finally, after the silence began to feel a bit long, I asked, "Is everything okay?"

"Yes."

I continued to wait, without saying a word.

"I think God wants us to bring you home from work."

My eyes widened. *What? Those are the same words he spoke at the house, but now I'm hearing them from work.*

The words "God wants us" stood out to me. I don't remember if I said anything or not, but he repeated the same words again. When he spoke this time, it was different. This time the words came from a place of brokenness, desperation, and humility. It was his emotions that got my attention. I didn't know what to say except, "Okay, we can talk about this more when I get home." But I knew. I knew what was about to happen.

God's Idea, Not Mine

I am about to leave my job. My career. The only employment that I've known since college.

As soon as I hung up the telephone, there was no delay. I walked straight out of my office and up the stairs to my supervisor, who was still the Director of Court Services and my friend. I walked into her office.

"I hate to bother you, but I need to talk with you."

She wasn't expecting me, but she made herself available, and I got right to the point.

"I don't think I'm going to be working here much longer."

I can only imagine what she thought in that moment because neither of us had ever had any conversations about me leaving.

"Is everything okay?" she asked.

I told her about the phone call I'd received just moments earlier. "There's something different about this phone call. The emotions behind my husband's words are out of character for him. I haven't seen him like this before. It has to be God. I think God's moving inside him."

I paused briefly. "If I don't leave work, then I'm not honoring what God is saying and what He's doing in my husband's life."

She just listened. Three months later, trusting God, I left my job of eighteen years.

My last day of work was in June, and Paige was out of school for the summer. After my husband left for work, it was just the two of us again, Paige and me.

We're going to the park!

When we got there, instead of being full of joy, I was a bit dazed. *What just happened to my life?* Work had always been very fulfilling to me. I don't mind working. In fact, I feel fully alive when I'm at work. I like the challenges, the feelings of accomplishment, the people, and the relationships. But now, I was home.

With Paige by my side, I looked around the playground, thinking, *Who wouldn't want this? Who wouldn't want to have what I have, to be able to stay at home and not work?* I knew I'd made the right decision. I knew I'd received a good thing, but I didn't know what to do with myself. I didn't know how to pass this time. I felt lost.

This became more obvious in the following days when I recognized that going to the mailbox to see if there was any mail had become the highlight of my day. *Something must be wrong with me. Everyone else thinks I should be happy. Why am I not happy about my new set of circumstances?*

Here I was again, exploring my thoughts and feelings. *What's going on here? Why am I feeling this way?* I began to see that a lot of my identity had come through my job, my career. I'd taken care of Paige for ten years, but apparently work had made a bigger impression on my identity than anything else. *I'm not sure who I am without my job.* This awareness caused me to ask more questions about how I saw myself. *Who am I away from work?* In asking this question, I was starting to see that I'm more than who I'd known myself to be. I began to see and to know that I'm more than my job. Any job.

Not only did my perception of my identity change—my perception of being at home also changed. I realized I wasn't esteeming the gift I'd received from God and my husband, the gift to be home with Paige. Once again, instead of feeling like I'd lost something, I began to realize I'd received another blessing.

By choosing to trust God and leaving my career, He was able to help me to let go of my old identity and to embrace the new thing He was doing in my life. God was showing me I could trust Him to give me a greater quality of life with Paige.

And, yes, God did give me a greater quality of life with Paige. In fact, it began before I came home from work.

Paige was four years old when I began noticing there was no change in her color or breathing when she was off oxygen for short periods of time, such as when taking a bath, getting dressed, and so on. I mentioned this to the pulmonologist at our regular appointment.

"We can take the oxygen off for twenty minutes to see how she does," he said.

I was like, "Okay."

Twenty minutes passed, and the nurse returned to check her oxygen saturation. The next thing I knew, we were going home without oxygen. Paige was fine! But the pulmonologist had one condition: "I still want her to have it at night."

That's nothing. After three years, today is the day we no longer need to carry a tank with us everywhere we go!

Out and About

Blessed shall you be when you come in, and blessed shall you be when you go out. (Deut. 28:6)

Although today Paige is both mentally and physically challenged, she's been taken everywhere her entire life. In her earliest years, when I didn't know how many days we would have with her, I purposed to have her live her days on this earth to their fullest. I didn't allow any challenging life event to keep us from participating, and I looked for ways to overcome any obstacle by making modifications. As a result, Paige hasn't missed out on anything she's wanted to be involved in.

In her early years, I took Paige to the park, the zoo, museums, bike riding, swimming, movies, the grocery store, shopping, church—you name it, I took her.

As she grew older, she went to summer camp, experienced motorized cars, Six Flags over Texas, Vacation Bible School, horseback riding, putt-putt, bowling, a gym membership, sleepovers with friends, and birthday parties.

Paige has traveled, gone to various festivals, hiked with me on my back, been white water rafting and zip lining—the sky's the limit! We've had to overcome an oxygen tank and physical limitations, but if there was a way to make it happen, it happened. Although I've been the forerunner in most of these things, my husband was always very willing and involved as well.

Early Years

During my initial leave of absence, one of the first places I took Paige was the duck pond near our home where we fed the ducks. I helped Paige tear off pieces of bread then showed her how to throw. It was fun and a bit exciting to see how close the ducks would get to us. They'd surround us with their quacking and honking just for a piece of bread.

After the duck pond, I began to find a variety of parks and events where we could walk outside. During those times, we weren't in a hurry but would take in everything going on around us, the sights and the sounds and the encounters with various people.

Still enjoying the outside, I began bicycle riding with Paige. I've always enjoyed bicycle riding, so my husband and I decided to get a bicycle carrier for Paige to go with me. We'd ride, ride, and ride some more! She enjoyed the movement, and the bumps made her laugh.

"Out and about" has given Paige the opportunity to see things she wouldn't normally have seen at home. The blue minivan was the first gift I knew she wanted. Paige saw it at a toy store. She kept touching me to get my attention and pointed to it. When I looked up and saw the blue minivan, I knew: *She wants this. Where'd she get this idea?*

On Paige's third birthday, the blue minivan rolled into the den, and her face lit up with excitement and delight. She still remembers this minivan, and the desire to have it hasn't changed. With our hearts full of joy over her enthusiasm, we placed her inside. She couldn't move the van with her legs, but she could move the steering wheel around. No one cared what she could or couldn't do—it didn't matter—she was happy!

Until the blue minivan, I never knew how much Paige was taking in from being "out and about." This event allowed me to see that she was having thoughts and feelings about what she was seeing.

It was more than a blue minivan. I'd caught a glimpse of Paige's heart.

Growing Older

Paige was about five years old when we came across a merry-go-round. It didn't have the typical horses—instead it had cars to sit in, and Paige wanted to ride in one of those cars. Although she didn't have the words to express what she wanted, she was persistent, pointing with determination. This time, her desire was actually stretching me. Knowing more about that merry-go-round than she did, I wasn't sure how she was going to react to the sudden movement when it started or went around and around. I was also wondering what to do if she wanted to get off before it stopped.

We decided to give it a go, and I placed her inside one of the cars and stepped away. The merry-go-round started to move, and the cars went around and around—and to my surprise she loved it! Using her limited sign language skills, she signed the word *more*! She knew what she wanted. She wasn't afraid, and she loved it. This experience opened up a whole new world. Yes, we jumped from a merry-go-round to roller coasters. It wasn't long before we bought season passes to the amusement park Six Flags over Texas because Paige loved the rides!

Two years later when Paige was seven, the Barbie Jeep arrived. Until then, Paige had been totally dependent on me and others for any movement beyond the walls of our home. At the age of four, while only able to scoot and roll around the floor, she'd received her first walker. Although she was able to walk with the walker, she didn't go far. Little did we know that the pink Barbie Jeep was going to open a door of greater independence for Paige.

It seemed like a good gift idea, but I wasn't sure how this battery-operated Jeep was going to work. There was no way of knowing if Paige would be able to understand how to get it moving, much less steer and drive it, but we bought it anyway.

Outside on the driveway, I placed her inside the Jeep and showed her the pedal on the floor. I positioned her foot over the pedal and said, "Push!" while putting some pressure on her knee to help her understand what I was saying. She got the idea and put her foot on the pedal and pushed, but she quickly let go. We practiced this over and over until she understood the concept, and then she took off!

She was in motion—out of the driveway and into the cul-de-sac! I knew she didn't have any control over where she was going, so I bolted after her and started running beside her, shouting, "This way! This way, Paige! Turn the wheel this way!" She understood and turned the wheel. Then I ran to the other side of the Jeep and said, "This way! This way, Paige! Turn the wheel this way!" She understood and turned the wheel this way.

I did this over and over again until Paige learned how to drive the Barbie Jeep. She knew how to make it go, and she knew how to make it stop. I was so proud of her. She got better and better, relying less and less on my directives. With me running beside her, she eventually learned to drive the Jeep all around our neighborhood.

For the first time, I saw other children come running alongside Paige and taking an interest in her. When she was in this Jeep, she appeared like them, and it made my heart rejoice.

Paige also enjoyed numerous family gatherings and hanging out with her cousins, whether it was for trick or treat, birthday parties, VBS, or summer camp at Granny and Grandpa's house. Since she's the only child, her cousins became more like brothers and sisters.

Elementary School

While Paige was still in elementary school, she let us know in her own way that she wanted to go skating for her birthday. I'm not sure how she came up with this idea, but we made it happen. I went to our local skating rink and talked with them about Paige being in a wheelchair (she uses this out in the community) and her desire to have a skating party for her birthday. They didn't see a problem with this request, so we invited her buddies from school. None of her buddies were part of the Special Education program—they were regular education peers. It surprised me that everyone invited wanted to come to Paige's skating party. What was even better was that they all wanted to push Paige in her wheelchair around the skating rink.

Middle School

Both at school and at church, there were a couple of girls who'd taken an interest in Paige. I saw this interest as an opportunity for Paige to have friends; therefore I purposed to get the girls together to do fun things with her. We did makeup and nails, baked cookies, went swimming, had sleepovers, ate pizza, popped popcorn, and even went "out and about" together. We went to the movies, the mall, and various eating establishments. I say "we" because I was always in the

> "Paige has a lot of motivation; which I believe she gets from her mom. She doesn't know her limits, because she hasn't had limits put on her." —Mrs. Regal, Middle School Teacher

> "Paige's favorite exclamation has always been "More!" Her sweet and courageous spirit drives her to live out this word for God and the world to see." —Mrs. LeBlanc, Middle School Teacher

mix. Since the girls were all still young, I wasn't sure how Paige would've had these experiences without me. I wanted her to enjoy what it was like to have friends.

I've also wanted Paige to fit in as much as possible, and I've tried to dress her in current fashion. Kids notice. People notice. It's not clothes that make a person or how much they cost, but the natural tendency is to notice those things that are different about someone. Clothes don't need to be one of those things.

I'd ask around, "What are girls this age wearing? What kinds of things do they like? What's in style or popular right now?" Paige couldn't tell me those things, so I advocated for her.

Paige was in middle school when she was nominated and selected "Student of the Month." They told us that this is a high honor where students are reviewed and selected on the basis of several areas, such as character. This gave Paige recognition, because they placed her name on the sign board in front of the school for several days.

Life in the Community

Over several years, Paige had many therapy appointments, including physical therapy, occupational therapy, and speech therapy. She also did therapeutic horseback riding. These all became a part of our routine. As Paige got older, she transitioned out of most of those programs, which is when I started taking her to a gym.

I stopped by a gym near our home one day and spoke with the manager when Paige was with me. I told him I'd like for Paige to walk on the treadmill and lift some weights. He listened to me, looked at Paige, and said, "I'm going to give her a VIP membership. She'll never have to pay as long as I'm here!" We had just received favor, something that continues to this day.

I began taking her to the gym a couple of days a week, where she walked on the treadmill and lifted weights. She enjoyed her time there, and people noticed. They watched Paige as she walked at a snail's pace on the treadmill. They watched her pushing and pulling weights on some of the machines. A few people came up to us and told me how watching Paige had inspired them. One person said, "After seeing her do what she's doing, I don't have anything to complain about." Paige was being an example to others just by living an overcoming life.

Travel

Paige has flown on a regular basis, beginning with the flight to Chicago. Even during the years when she was on oxygen twenty-four hours a day, we traveled. Since she still uses oxygen at night, we travel with a portable machine. Over the years, I've made arrangements for oxygen on the airplane, in the hotel, and for pickups and drop-offs. We travel with her walker and a fold-up stroller as well. And we also take a portable nebulizer machine for breathing treatments—whatever it takes. None of these things has stopped us from traveling.

During our travels, Paige has found herself on my back during a three-mile hike up the side of a mountain to a beautiful lake in Montana, and again to the top of Diamond Head in Hawaii. Fear didn't keep us from putting Paige on a raft so she could experience white water rafting. And fear hasn't kept us from letting her ride an inner tube behind a boat.

Paige has been to Italy twice. The first time we went, I never gave it a second thought. It looked like a fun trip, so we went. Paige has seen the Leaning Tower of Pisa with one of her favorite drinks in her hand, Dr. Pepper. She has been to the Coliseum in Rome. She has seen the Michelangelo David.

Like the poem about Holland said, I did turn my eyes from Italy when Paige was first born to start looking for the tulips in Holland. Now as I look back, I realize we'd never gone to Holland, and in fact my life with Paige was being lived in Italy. We've experienced everything that Italy had to offer.

The poem "Welcome to Holland" did help me though. It spoke to me almost thirty years ago when I truly needed it. However, our life is not any slower than life in Italy. Our life is not any less beautiful than life in Italy. We've lived everything that Italy has to offer. I'm sure Holland has beautiful windmills and tulips, but I didn't end up going to the wrong destination. I made it to the right destination—the one God had for me all along.

Graduation

Today, I'm sitting in a big auditorium with many other parents and students because today Paige is graduating from high school. There are well over seven hundred students and thousands of family and friends. All the students are wearing caps and gowns. As I sit here, they're beginning to call out the names listed in the program. Paige's name is closer to the end.

One by one, people are cheering as their loved one walks across the stage. I wait and wait as they call out other names. I keep looking at the program to find Paige's name, somehow thinking that this will make the process go faster.

Now I see Paige leave the row of chairs she's been sitting in. She's getting into position. The announcer is getting closer to her name in the bulletin. I realize that in a blink of an eye what has taken many years to accomplish is about to be recorded in history.

And now the moment is here. I hear the name of the baby girl I gave birth to, my daughter who has overcome so much. My daughter who was not supposed to live. I hear the announcer call out the name "Paige Richardson."

Tears filling my eyes, I watch her coming across the stage. Mrs. Alvarado, a special teacher and friend is pushing her in her wheelchair. Paige is about to receive her high school diploma! I try to seal this moment forever in my memory. I see Paige reach her hand out to receive her diploma! With cheers and applause from many, we all stand, celebrating this moment in time.

Later this day, there's another big party at the house. The house is full of family and friends coming and going as we celebrate this accomplishment in Paige's life—an accomplishment not so much of school but of her accomplishment of life.

After overcoming a life that was brutal to her for the first few years, Paige has turned into a

> "She will always have a special place in my heart! Like so many, I love your daughter. She has taught me so much." —Mrs. Alvarado, High School Teacher

beautiful person inside and out. Over the years, her body and heart have healed. She has a family who loves her, and she loves being around people.

Although she's physically and mentally challenged, she has many interests. She loves music, horseback riding, and going out and about, and she's always up for *more*! Most of all, her smile, laugh, and big brown eyes light up any room.

This day we are celebrating moments upon moments, memories upon memories, of living life with Paige.

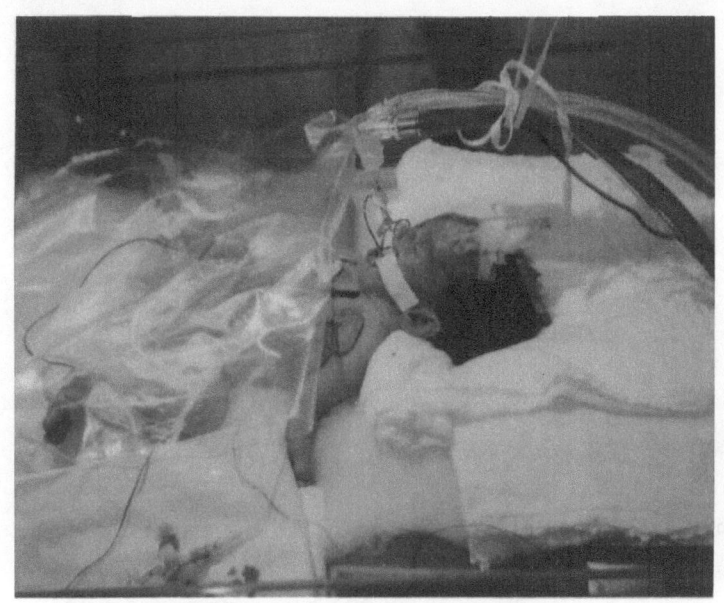

Paige at three days old after her first surgery

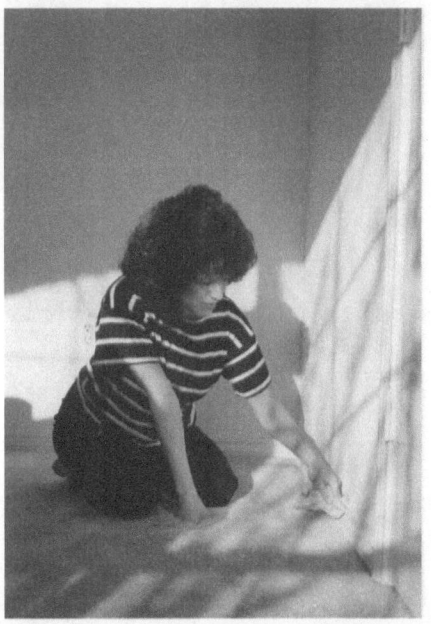

Preparing the baby's room before Paige was born

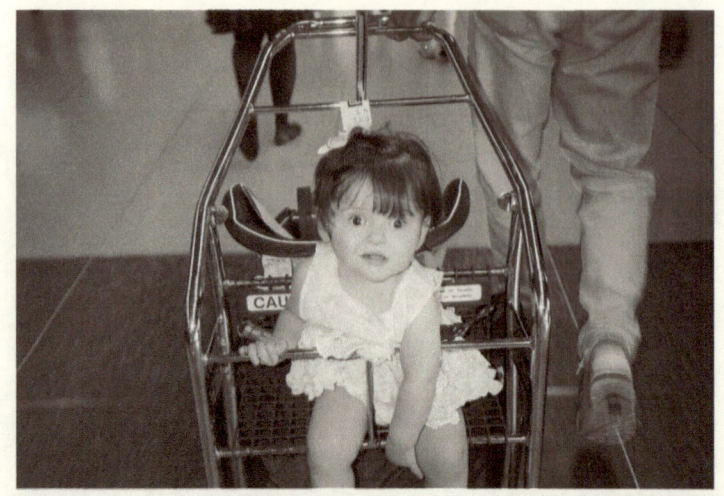

Paige at eighteen months, in the Chicago airport headed to the hospital

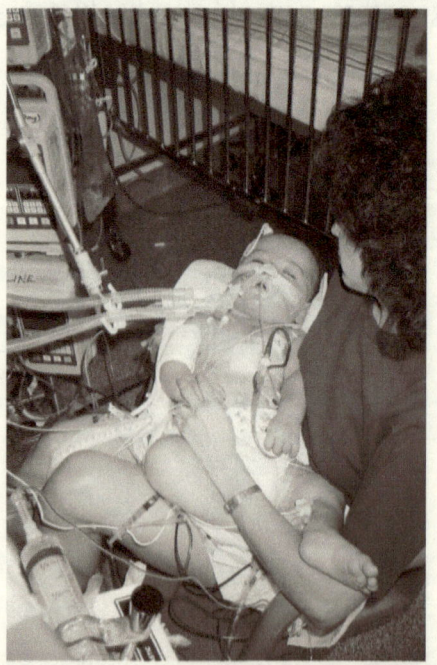

Sharon and Paige in Chicago, not knowing if Paige would survive

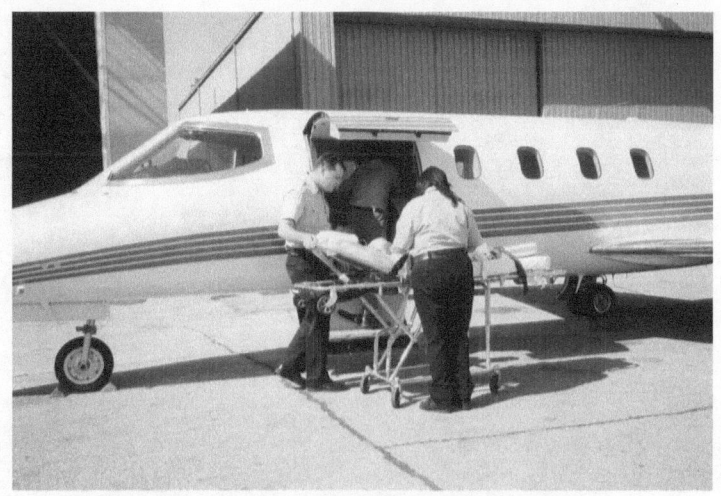

Medical flight from Chicago back to Texas

Sharon holding on to Paige after hearing the doctor's words, "Time will tell."

An early photo of going *out and about* with Paige

Paige at seven years in her Barbie Jeep

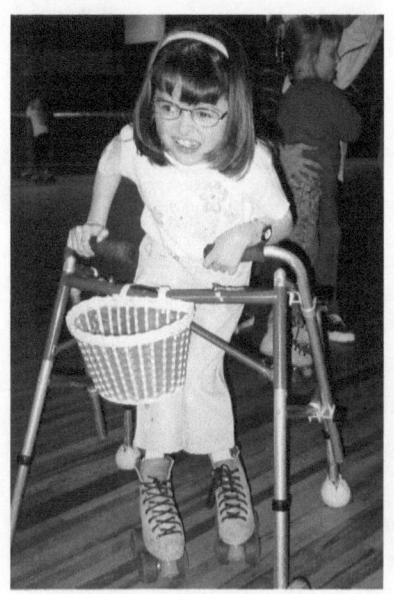

Paige at ten years at her skating party

Paige at twelve, hiking with Mom to the summit of Diamond Head in Hawaii

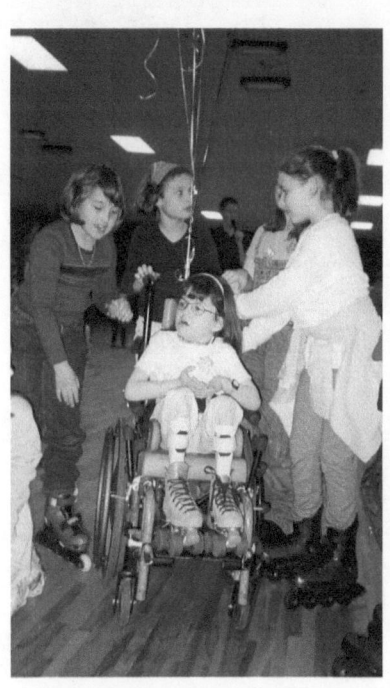

Paige with her friends at the skating party

Paige at fifteen with two of her closest friends

Sharon and Paige on one of our adventures

Paige at twenty-three, swinging from a vine with Mom's help

Enjoying a rare snow in Texas

Paige's first trip to Italy, age fourteen, in front of the Leaning Tower of Pisa

Paige's second trip to Italy, age twenty-six, with traveling friend Babe Laufenberg

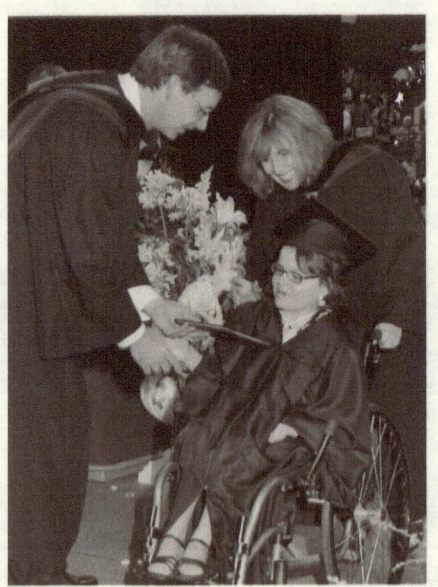

Paige's high school graduation, with one of her favorite teachers, Mrs. Alvarado

The Cousins

"Life with Paige is having a best friend, a cheerleader, and a support system all combined into one smiling cousin. Her energy and positive attitude are encouraging and contagious. Her heart is focused not only on the Lord but on everyone she meets. Life with Paige is never lonely. I have my sleepover buddy, movie buddy, shopping buddy, and karaoke buddy all combined into one. I love to hear the sweet echo of 'just like Chandler'! Life with Paige is fun, and I wouldn't trade it for the world." —**Chandler**

"A special memory I have of Paige is when we were visiting Grannie and Grandpa. We had all gone out with Grandpa as he towed us across the land with his four-wheeler. We hit a rocky/dirt patch and the trailer toppled over and all of the grand kids went flying out, all except Paige. Paige was still sitting in the same spot, almost wedged in safe and sound. She couldn't stop laughing causing all of us to laugh with her. That's one beautiful thing Paige has always given us, the ability to laugh despite any hardships we may be facing. She may not quite understand the full extent of everything, but part of me believes that she's more aware than she can let on, and laughter is her way of saying, 'Things are all good.'" —**Robby**

"I have always looked up to you, Aunt Sharon, with how well you have taken care of Paige. Some people would see her as a burden, but you always saw her as a blessing! That is one of the most inspiring things I've ever seen. No matter the struggles you've faced, you always met them with your head up and a smile on your face. You are one of the strongest women I know.

"Paige has always been one to light up a room! When she smiles, it makes everyone around her want to smile." —**Christopher**

The Aunts and Uncle

"Sharon is the reason why Paige has accomplished so much through her lifetime. Sharon's determination and love for Paige helped her to accomplish things that the doctors said Paige could never do, like walk, talk, or eat. Paige beat all the odds. Sharon's strong faith and love for God got her through all of Paige's trials and tribulations. Sharon has never treated Paige like she has a disability. She has raised her to be as normal as anyone else.

"I also love Paige's spirit. Over the years Paige has learned to have her own relationship with God. She now loves to share that with others and pray for them. Paige has the best life because she doesn't judge others, she loves everyone regardless. Paige does not hate because she doesn't know how, she only knows how to show love. Paige is the closest replication of God as you can get. After all, He did make her in His image." —**Christi/Sister**

"Paige is a true gift from God; no one can deny that. Paige loves to share her love for God with everyone she meets. She knows no strangers. Some may think she doesn't understand, however that's not true, she knows everything that we talk about and has feelings just like any other young lady her age." —**Chica/Sister-in-Law**

"You have done a tremendous job with Paige. I'm sure she wouldn't be with us if it wasn't for you. You are the angel on earth and Paige is the miracle. I love you both." —**Eric/Brother**

The Divorce

Therefore, what God has joined together, let not man separate.
Mark 10:9

As I HUNG UP the telephone, I heard a voice in my head say, "This is going to be a really bad year." I just stood there. *That's odd. Where did that come from?* At first, it wasn't the meaning of the words that seemed odd—it was how clearly I heard that voice. It was as if a person had just spoken in my head. *What's this voice saying?* I'd heard God at various times—when He told me about Paige being a gift and when He encouraged me through Scripture—but this voice was very clear and appeared to be telling me about my future. I wasn't familiar with this. *So odd.*

My husband was sitting nearby and noticed I hadn't moved one inch since I'd hung up the telephone. "Who was that on the phone?" he said.

I told him who it was, and then I told him what I'd heard in my head. He listened intently, but he wasn't as intrigued about the message or the voice. Instead, he gave me words of reassurance.

"Oh, Sharon, I'm sure everything is going to be just fine."

"I guess so," I replied. So in spite of feeling intrigued by it and a bit puzzled, I shook it off, choosing not to think about it anymore and to go on with my day. What I didn't know was, it *was* going to be "a really bad year."

Nine months later, my youngest brother who was only thirty-seven years old passed away suddenly. And I was in the midst of a marriage crisis no one knew about. In the midst of these things happening, I had no remembrance of the clear voice or of the words I'd heard in my head at the beginning of the year—the words that seemed to be telling me about my future. I was too focused on trying to keep it all together.

Days before Christmas, my husband of eighteen years left our home. The day he left I wasn't thinking about the words he'd spoken to me at the beginning of the year, when I didn't move after hanging up the phone—the words that had felt so reassuring to me: "Oh, Sharon, I'm sure everything is going to be just fine."

Everything wasn't fine. Life as I'd known it was changing drastically. Shock and unbelief filled me—including loss and sorrow, numbness and confusion. Familiar words from long ago entered my thoughts: *This has to be someone else's life. Surely not mine.*

His leaving deeply pierced my heart, and brokenness settled in quickly. I had no idea how I was going to navigate through this. My head spun, filling up with all kinds of thoughts and questions. *What's my family going to think about all of this?* Our family hadn't even healed from the loss of my brother, just three months ago. *My parents! They're still grieving the sudden death of one of their children, and now I'm going to bring more grief and sadness to them because of my life. And how in the world can I face our friends?*

There'd been no sign of problems in our marriage. *How am I going to be able to walk through the doors of our church?* On the outside, our family had it all together. *What just happened to my life?* I was in total disbelief. *Oh, my! What about Paige? What about her life?* Filled with great sorrow, I felt very alone.

The Divorce

Sitting in the den of our home in complete brokenness, I thought about Paige. *I need to keep it together for Paige. She doesn't need to feel the impact of what's going on in my heart. Somehow I need to protect her from feeling all the sadness I'm feeling right now. Her world doesn't need to change because of my emotions.* As far as she knew, her world hadn't changed. It was the Christmas season, a season that we celebrate, and she was out of school on Christmas break.

I set out to do just that—to celebrate Christmas. The first thing I did was to get Paige into the car to go look at Christmas lights. It was all I could do to drive her around, but I did it for her. I drove through various neighborhoods, pointing toward the Christmas lights that stood out to me—the grand ones and the ones full of beauty. I wanted Paige to see them. I didn't want her to miss anything.

As I looked over to the seat next to me, I saw Paige's face. *She's filled with so much joy and delight, so sweet and innocent.* Searching my heart, I knew, *She's going to be seeing my reaction to the events happening in my life. She's going to be able to sense my joy or sadness. How I navigate through this has the potential to cause this joy to go away.* It was very clear to me that I had a beautiful heart entrusted into my care.

God had always entrusted me with the care and protection of Paige's heart. I cared for it when she first came home from the hospital by creating an atmosphere of peace and telling her how much I loved her. After more trauma, I helped her heart trust again by giving more love and speaking life over her. She's had a lifetime of this from me and others. Her heart was now full of life. I didn't want to see any of this go away. *I need to help protect her heart.*

Christmas being just days away, I knew I needed to tell my immediate family. We were all facing the reality of my brother not being with us that Christmas, nor at any other Christmas, and the emptiness and sadness that came with it. We hadn't talked about it much because it was difficult to talk about. But it was obvious everyone in their own way was coping with the difficulty of that Christmas season. I knew that after hearing my news, our family would have to grieve a marriage that was falling apart as well as mourn my brother's death.

It wasn't easy, but I did tell my family. Somehow we made it through Christmas that year. However, it didn't take me long to realize that this journey was bigger than me and my aching heart. Just because my family now knew what was going on in my life, it didn't change my situation. They were desperate, just as I was, to see me in a better place, yet they couldn't do anything except encourage me. This was my journey. I was the only one responsible for making me better.

At first it felt as if my emotions were filling up time. Seconds seemed like days—minutes seemed like months—days felt like they would never end, and yet not one day had even passed. Some days it was all that I could do to get up in the morning. But I didn't just have myself to take care of—I had Paige.

One afternoon I looked toward the kitchen table and saw Paige sitting there gazing out the window, and I knew immediately what was going on. In that moment, I realized, *I can't protect Paige from my reality any longer. There's no way I can isolate her from what's going on in the marriage.*

Paige doesn't know how to tell time from a clock, but she does have an internal clock. This internal clock is accustomed to routine. This was about the time Daddy would be coming home. She was sitting in her chair, looking out the window like she always did, waiting for him to drive into the driveway.

What I knew she didn't know was on that day, and in the days to come, that he probably wasn't going to be driving into the driveway. And as I stood there looking at her, I was reminded again that I had another heart to take care of. I might not have been able to protect her from everything that was happening, but I could help protect her heart. Still, I wondered, *What does that look like? How do I steward her heart through this season?*

One would think the surprise of Paige's birth with all of the complications and challenges that went with it wouldn't have begun to compare to this, but somehow this seemed much bigger. This was the second time in my life when I was required to draw upon the deposits inside me.

I started searching, but I was very cautious navigating through this unchartered territory. This time I went straight to God and waited on Him to show me what to do.

"God, I need your help. I don't know how to do this," I prayed. "I don't have a clue. I feel so alone. I feel so isolated. How am I ever going to dig out of this? Who am I going to tell? What do I say? I have a lot of friends, but who am I supposed to share this with?"

I've known God, and He's shown up for me off and on throughout my life. But I'd heard about people who "hear from God" on a regular basis. Until now, I hadn't experienced God like this. Now I wanted to. The first thing I heard was the word *honor*. I felt like I'd been given instructions to honor.

Honor her father. But what does that look like?

The next time I saw Paige looking out the window, I spoke to her. "Are you waiting for Daddy?"

"Yes."

"I don't think Daddy's coming home right now, but I know he loves you. I know Daddy loves you very much. He loves his girl."

And when I'd see her looking for him again, that day or on another day, I'd say to her, "Do you miss Daddy?"

When she replied yes, I'd say to her, "I'm so sorry you miss your daddy. I know you love him very much. I know he loves you too."

Then we would pray for Daddy. Many times after doing this, I'd go into the other room and cry. It wasn't easy, but I honored him and cared for Paige's heart.

I soon discovered some hidden feelings about doing this. I didn't have peace. So I got alone and began searching *my* heart. *I want to see if I can figure out what these feelings are about.* I began picturing different scenarios in my mind, various things that had happened. As I thought about the event, if it didn't have any effect on me, I'd think about another event. I kept doing this until I reached an event that stung. Then I'd stop and ask, *Why is this bothering me?* As I continued asking myself more questions, I discovered what was really bothering me.

I discovered I'm actually more okay that my husband's actions affected me, but I'm not okay that those same actions affected Paige. My heart was broken at the thought of Paige not having both parents living with her. I'd been proud at times of the fact that her life had been different up until then, than that of so many other children with special needs. She had both parents loving and living with her. She was still loved, but now she wasn't living with both parents, which God never intended. The impact of our troubled marriage on her bothered me because she was an innocent bystander, and she hadn't done anything to deserve this.

What do I do with these feelings? I wondered. I kind of wanted to hold on to them, but I knew it wasn't what I was supposed to do. I had a choice. I knew I needed to forgive.

What does forgiveness look like?

Forgiveness is not a feeling. It's a choice. Forgiveness doesn't mean you agree with the action that occurred. It also doesn't mean you are excusing the action. What it does mean is that we get to choose to let go of the feelings we have toward someone because the feelings are only affecting us. Our feelings are not doing anything to the other person. If I choose to hold onto those feelings, they will only poison me. If I hold onto unforgiveness, it will only hurt me. Forgiving is actually a gift I give to myself.

I did choose to forgive, but there were still times when I found myself feeling sad about how this was affecting Paige. It was a process. I always had the choice to go back into unforgiveness, but I continued to choose to forgive. I chose to do this for me. Once I forgave, I felt like God asked me to pray for her dad. So I did. I prayed for him and asked God to bless him. I didn't do this for any other reason than knowing it was the right thing to do. I knew that God told me to honor him, and He told me to pray. This process of forgiveness benefited me; it helped heal my heart.

Navigating life with Paige was only one aspect of this abrupt change in my life. For many years now, we'd attended church regularly and had a lot of friends. Church is like an extension of my family; however, I didn't know who I could talk to. The one thing that came to me was not to say anything to anyone. My desire was to keep my husband covered. *Love covers, right?* That seemed like the right thing to do. In my mind, love covered him, but love also covered us. I believed this would all go away, that he'd come back, and we wouldn't have to tell anyone. I knew what to do. I wasn't going to say anything to anyone. I felt equipped to go to church.

Although I felt equipped, I had to make myself walk through the doors of our church. I knew I had instructions to cover, but I soon realized it was me I wanted covered. I kept thinking that everyone must see the word "separated" or "divorcing" over my head. I walked through the doors with Paige and without my husband. Wondering how I was going to interact with everyone, I quickly realized it was a challenge to my identity.

Here I go again. What's going on for me?

After church, I got alone with God. I wanted to ask Him about what happened at church. *God, what is this I'm feeling?* And as I listened, I felt like God said to me in a still small voice, "Do you know your identity? Do you know where your identity comes from? Does it come from man or from God? Are you concerned about what man thinks of you, or about what I say about you?" Yes, this was definitely about my identity.

What does my identity look like?

During this time, God revealed that my identity doesn't come from a person or from what the world says, but from who God says I am. I realized I have no control over someone else's life and the choices or decisions they make. It doesn't mean their choices and decisions don't have a direct impact on me because they do, but they don't define me.

I felt like God was saying, "Being married is only one aspect of who you are." Just like I'm a daughter, I'm a sister, I'm a friend, I'm a mom. These are only different aspects of who I am, but each one individually does not define me. I am much more than a person who is married. God says I have great value and great worth. I'm a good person. I'm a kind person. I am full of love. I am loveable. All the years of who I've known myself to be don't go away just because of an event in my life. These truths flooded my thoughts. *God is helping me. He's the one who's reminding me who I am and who He is.*

But how does this help me move forward?

It did help me. The next time I walked through the doors of my church, I remembered that my identity is in who God says I am, not in who man says I am. It didn't matter what people thought about my situation. God knew what was going on, and God knew my heart.

Our family was well known at this church, so it wasn't like I could go hide in the back of the sanctuary. Again, choosing to hold my head high, I walked inside the doors of the church with the confidence and grace God poured over me. Joy and happiness filled me as I interacted with all the beautiful people I'd known over the years. There was no shame.

> My grace is sufficient for you, for My strength is made perfect in weakness. (2 Cor. 12:9)

What was remarkable to me was that several Sundays passed before anyone noticed my husband was missing. And if they did notice, they didn't say anything. Maybe I *was* being covered. The first time someone did ask, I honored. *Honor does not speak negatively against the other person.* Therefore the words I spoke were not negative. *Honor seeks the highest good for that other person.* I asked others to lift me up in prayer. *Honor is restorative and does not tear down.* If the person asking was one of my husband's close friends, I suggested they reach out to him.

Choose honor.

Honoring others allows you to keep walking with perseverance into situations that seem impossible to walk into, which turns into grace upon grace and keeps peace in your heart.

Time began to pass. Although most people didn't know the full story, church seemed to be going okay for Paige and me. I was happy about this; however there was another group of people with whom I was learning to navigate this difficult season.

I now attended BSF, the same study my husband was in at the time God brought me home from work. After I left my career, I was able to fit this into my schedule. As a result of attending BSF, the Bible became alive. For the first time in my life, the Scriptures I read began to have meaning. And for the first time in my life, I loved my Bible.

I was now in my seventh year of attending BSF. Each week in our small groups we'd have the opportunity to submit prayer requests. I didn't usually submit prayer requests, but I felt like I needed additional reinforcement, so I asked the group to pray for my husband. They didn't know the details—they just knew to pray for him. God knew the details. I kept him covered.

Over the course of fifteen months, I stood for the marriage. I prayed for it. I fasted. I did everything I felt God asked me to do. And although I was experiencing God in a way I'd never experienced before in my life, it was becoming apparent the marriage wasn't reconciling. In fact, it was going in the opposite direction—my marriage was ending. God was even speaking to me about letting go of the hope of restoration.

Although this grieved me deeply, God reminded me that He is always working on my behalf, and His heart's desire is for people to stay married. I believed He had gone before me, and I trusted that He had given my husband and I the same opportunity to see Him do a miraculous work in our lives. But He was also showing me it takes two people seeking this. He was showing me that if only one person is moving in that direction, it just can't work. He grieves too. However, He was releasing me.

I wasn't in court the day it happened. I didn't want to be there, so I didn't go. I never knew the moment it happened. I felt God had kept me from that experience. In fact, I was out of town, visiting family in another state. That's the memory God left me with.

Back to Bible Study Fellowship. As I mentioned, my husband had been on the prayer list, and my friends had prayed and prayed and prayed. Since I was now divorced, I thought it was probably time to take him off this list. They didn't know I was divorced, and I realized I didn't want them to know—and it wasn't just them. I didn't really want to tell anyone.

Here I go again. What's this all about, God? What's going on with me? Is it that identity thing again? I knew I needed to get alone with

The Divorce

God and ask Him these questions, and during my time alone with Him, I discovered what was going on with me. Following is one of the journal entries I made:

> I'm discovering that speaking the words "I'm divorced" is difficult for me. Why is this? I've known that speaking these words is difficult, but now I'm finding that there's more to this. Once I speak these words, I won't be able to keep this personal failure private. I'll be exposing my lack of perfection to the world. What will they think of me? Will they still love me? Will they reject me? I'm having thoughts of feeling less than and possibly losing friends.

It was after I journaled this that God reminded me none of it is true. He reminded me that I wasn't a failure, and people would still love me; I wouldn't be rejected, and I'd still have friends. This was the truth I desired to embrace!

Two months later, I had an opportunity to do this on the last day of BSF in May. Traditionally, the last day is known as "Share Day." Share Day is a day where you get up in front of everyone and share what God has done in your life during the year. You give a testimony.

When the invitation came, I thought, *I've never been to Share Day. In seven years, I've never been.* Thinking more about it, I concluded, *I think I'll go! It might be fun to see what this is all about!* And then another thought came: *Am I supposed to share on Share Day? Oh no!* I knew where this was going. Getting up in front of people has not been "my thing." But I got a strong impression God was asking me to do something that would make me feel uncomfortable.

"God, if you want me up there, then show me what you want me to share."

And He did.

The following week I found myself standing in front of at least four hundred women and giving my testimony—the testimony of how I'd found myself in the middle of a divorce after eighteen years of marriage. I shared with these women my journey of healing and how God had walked with me through the fire, and how I was now on the other side. I told them I desired complete healing and that God had shown me an area where I was not healed.

I shared that I couldn't say the word divorce. I said, "I don't like this word. God doesn't like this word. It's not God's perfect will. It's not who I am in Christ, but it's part of my story. I know that I need to be able to say this word." After saying this, I stood in front of all of those women and said the words that had been holding me captive. I took a deep breath and said, "I'm divorced." Nothing changed in that moment, but I said what had been so difficult to say.

God was setting me free. And freedom feels good!

If the Son makes you free, you shall be free indeed! (John 8:36)

Divorce is painful. Although God never intends for any marriage to end, He is faithful to make us whole again. That's what He did for me. I set out to go through that season with God. I journaled my thoughts, I read Scriptures on divorce, relationships, love, husbands and wives, pain, covenant, and so on. I learned. I grew, and He healed my heart. God showed me my identity. I learned to trust Him. He brought peace into my heart. He showed me when to move and when not to move. God took care of me and showed me how to steward Paige's heart. He showed me what it's like to be in relationship with Him, which is something I'd never known. This was the greatest gift of all. Now God calls me "His friend."

Abraham believed God, and it was accounted to him for righteousness. And he was called the friend of God. (James 2:23)

"Sharon believed God, and it was accounted to her for righteousness." And she is called a friend of God.

Three years had passed since I first heard the words in my head, "This is going to be a really bad year." Although it was a painful season, it was a good season. It was a season full of inspiration and growth. It was a season of loss and letting go. During this season, relationships changed. I lost some friends and gained new ones. My worship style changed. What I watched on TV changed. The music I listened to changed. My thoughts and actions were all a little different, in a good way. On New Year's Eve, the last journal entry I made that year was, "Thank You God for a different but *good* year!" *Thank You for this season in my life with Paige.*

The Word

*Indeed, I have spoken it; I will also bring it to pass.
I have purposed it; I will also do it.*
Isaiah 46:11

THERE WAS A WORD that changed my life. I thought it was just going to be an ordinary church picnic. Little did I know that a conversation I'd have that day was going to change the direction of my life. When I think about that day, I still see her face, the face of my new friend standing in front of me. I can also see the moment in our conversation when she hesitated. She had something to share with me, something she felt God was saying to her, yet she didn't know whether she was supposed to say anything or not.

During my season of divorce, God led me to a different church. I have no recollection of how I got to this church, but I do remember the first day I walked through the doors. This was a much larger church than the one I'd been attending. As I stood at the doorway looking into the sanctuary, my first thought was, *This church is too big*. But I heard the Lord say, "It's not about the size of the church, it's about you and Me right now." In this season of my life, God led me to Gateway Church.

On this beautiful spring day in early April, Gateway Church was having their annual picnic to celebrate their volunteers. This year they'd located the picnic away from the busy city to a ranch on the outskirts of town. As Paige and I walked up, a greeting line of people giving us high fives welcomed us to the event. There were various activities going on everywhere. As I looked around, I saw kids jumping inside bounce houses and people throwing horseshoes. I heard numbers called out for bingo and chattering conversations while people ate barbeque.

Not ready to eat yet, I decided to push Paige around to see who and what we could find. I began talking with a few people; some I knew and some I didn't. Continuing to walk around the ranch, I saw Kim, who served on the altar ministry, and I remembered her because she'd prayed for me before. We walked over to where she was standing. I'd always enjoyed talking with her and being in her presence because she carries the Word of God in her. I also knew she had a prophetic gifting that God had been teaching me about. What I didn't know was that she would have "a word" for me today.

Our conversation was easy and very lighthearted as we got to know each other better. As the three of us talked, I noticed Kim would start to say something and then stop herself. Aware of this hesitation, I spoke up. "What are you thinking?"

"It may be too soon to share," she said.

Thoughts quickly went through my head. *I know she hears from God. I think she has a prophetic word for me. Yet it doesn't seem like she wants to share it with me. Maybe she doesn't think I'm going to be able to receive what she has to say.*

What Is Prophecy?

For those of you reading who may be unfamiliar with the prophetic gifting, one of the places where the Bible talks about it is in 1 Corinthians 14:1: "Pursue love, and desire spiritual gifts, but especially that you may prophesy."

When we prophecy, it is to strengthen and encourage the body of Christ (1 Cor. 14:3 NIV). Other translations use the words edification, exhortation, and comfort. First Corinthians 14:1 encourages everyone to desire this gift. If this gift is available, and it's God's idea, then He must want us to hear His voice. John 10:27 says, "My sheep hear My voice." The gift of prophecy is a way to share with someone what God is saying. The words can also be predictive of the future. Unlike horoscopes, palm readers, or psychics (which come from the wrong spirit), prophetic words come from God, who is love. If anyone receives a prophetic word and it does not feel edifying, encouraging, or strengthening, it didn't come from the heart of God. First John 4:1 says, "Beloved, do not believe every spirit, but test the spirits."

I had enough understanding of the prophetic gifting and trusted her, so I believed I was ready to hear what she had to say. "I don't think it's too soon. It's okay if you share."

She began to prophesy: "You will marry again. This man is going to be very strong in his faith. This man you marry will be instrumental in the healing of your daughter. God is going to heal her, and she will get out of this chair. It will glorify God and bring others to salvation."

I thought, *Okay, I know I'm going to get married again. I do know that. This isn't really new information to me. But Paige being healed and getting up out of her chair is definitely a new concept.*

I chose my words to my new friend carefully. "I do know I'm going to get married again. But it's okay if you would like to pray for me about the other because I think Paige is perfect the way she is." I went on. "If God wants to heal her, that's fine with me, but He needs to change my heart because I love her just the way she is."

I was slightly baffled yet curious about it all and left the picnic pondering those words. Those words changed the direction of my life. *I sure don't know a God that wants to heal Paige. I mean, He's healed her through doctors and medicine, but I'm not sure about anything other than that. I know the Bible talks about healings, but I haven't seen anything like this in my life, nothing like what my friend is talking about.*

Here's my first journal entry after this experience:

> I've always accepted Paige for who she is, and I've thought (believed) that she has her own ministry because of who she is. She's glorified You, Lord, by just accepting her life. She has been an example to many. God, I am open to what You have planned for Paige and me. If it is to bring glory to You and bring many to salvation, we would love to be a part of this. It would be an honor and privilege for You to use us like this. It would be more than I can even imagine. I can imagine it, but to wrap the reality around it is another thing. Please God, if this is to be, give me the faith to bring it to fulfillment. Amen.

I didn't stop there. The next season of my life, I got into the Word of God to see what it says about healing. I went to the New Testament and read all of the Scriptures and stories about Jesus when He went around healing people.

One of the first Scripture verses that really spoke to me was John 9:1–2: "Now as Jesus passed by, He saw a man who was blind from birth. And His disciples asked Him, saying, 'Rabbi, who sinned, this man or his parents, that he was born blind?'" My heart leaped when I read this. I knew Paige wasn't blind, but she'd been like this since birth. The disciples assumed there was sin, and I thought, *Did I do something that caused Paige to be this way?*

Then I read the next verse, John 9:3. Jesus answered, "Neither this man nor his parents sinned, but that the works of God should be revealed in him." *Wow! Just Wow! I'm receiving something from this verse. Something's going on inside of me. I can feel it. I'm feeling relieved at Jesus's answer. He said, "This was not the parents' fault."*

I'd never really thought about it before, but I felt a sense of strength inside me. I was feeling vindicated. I hadn't done anything wrong. This passage helped me understand this man's blindness was no one's fault and healing is to glorify God. Jesus said, "So the works of God could be revealed."

"Thank You, God, that this is not my fault," I said. "Thank You for showing me that when things happen from birth that are out of our control, it's not anyone's fault. Thank You for showing me through Your Word that these are opportunities for You to be glorified, for people to see Your power at work in their lives. If this is what You said to me, then this must be what You have for all parents of children with special needs."

Another Scripture verse that spoke to me during this season was Acts 3:1–9, which I refer to as "The Beautiful Gate." It goes,

> Now Peter and John went up together to the temple at the hour of prayer, the ninth hour. And a certain lame man from his mother's womb was carried, whom they laid daily at the gate of the temple, which is called Beautiful, to ask alms from those who entered the temple; who, seeing Peter and John about to go into the temple, asked for alms. And fixing his eyes on him, with John, Peter said, "Look at us." So, he gave them his attention, expecting to receive something from them. Then Peter said, "Silver and gold I do not have, but what I do have I give you: In the name of Jesus Christ of Nazareth, rise up and walk." And he took him by the right hand and lifted him up and immediately his feet and ankle bones received strength. So he, leaping up, stood and walked and entered the temple with them—walking, leaping and praising God. And all of the people saw him walking and praising God.

How could someone who's been lame from his mother's womb be healed with four words? "Rise up and walk!" "Rise up and walk!" It seemed so simple. Something stirred inside me again, and I had a sudden thought: *This is Paige! This is how easy it can be for Paige!* Now I was getting very excited!

I continued to read more and more about the healings in the Bible, what Jesus did and what He said when people were healed. John 16:23–24 says, "Most assuredly I say to you, whatever you ask the Father in My name He will give you. Until now you have asked nothing in My name. Ask, and you will receive, that your joy may be full."

As I read this Scripture, I thought, *This verse says, "Until now, you have not asked for anything in My name."* I had asked God to heal Paige before. I wanted her out of the hospital. I wanted the doctors to intervene. I wanted them to do something with their knowledge, to heal Paige. I had asked God to keep her alive, and He had.

But now, to change her physical and mental status? To change the way her body looked? To have her walk without a walker? To have her walk straight and not have a twisted hip? For her back to be straight, free from the kyphosis that causes her to bend over? For her to be able to talk in a normal voice and have the mental capacity of someone her age or beyond? For her to be able to chew her food without ever having to cut it up again? For her lungs to be healed so she would never have respiratory issues again? To have her heart repaired supernaturally so she'd never need another surgery again—ever? No, I hadn't asked God to heal Paige like that.

I've always thought she's perfect the way she is. This is what God had told me when she was born. "Every good and perfect gift comes from above." Why would He be changing His mind now?

My searching continued. In addition to searching the Scriptures, I attended any teaching or conference where they were talking about healing. I wanted to know more about this type of healing. Although I knew God, I wanted to know more about this God who healed. I had believed Him for emotional healing and medical healing, but what about supernatural healing? I had so many questions. "Does He still do this today, or are these stories just for the Bible?"

Faith

As I continued reading these stories, I saw something many of them had in common—faith. *That's what it's all about. Healing can't happen without it.* So in my conversations with God, I told Him, "I want to see the power of my faith."

> If you have *faith* as a mustard seed, you will say to this mountain, "Move from here to there," and it will move and nothing will be impossible for you. (Matt. 17:20, emphasis mine)

> Be of good cheer, daughter, your *faith* has made you well. (Matt. 9:22, emphasis mine)

When the desire for my faith increased, my journal entries began to change. Journal entry:

> I believe that You are healing Paige from her chronic lung disease, heart disease, her muscles, joints, ligaments, tendons, her brain. Lord, Your Word says that faith is the only requirement for healing. I pray that I have at least the faith of a mustard seed, if not more. Give to me according to Your good pleasure. Thank You for what You are doing in my life.

Compassion

In further reading, I discovered that when Jesus healed the sick, He was "moved with compassion." Compassion is having sympathy and concern for others' misfortunes and desiring to help make them better. Jesus desired to help.

> And when Jesus went out, He saw a great multitude; and He was moved with *compassion* for them, and healed their sick. (Matt. 14:14, emphasis mine)

Power and Authority

I discovered that because of Jesus, we have power and authority to heal the sick. This power and authority is not just for the disciples but for all believers.

> Then He called His twelve disciples together and gave them *power and authority* over all demons, and to cure diseases. He sent them to preach the kingdom of God and to heal the sick. (Luke 9:1–2, emphasis mine)

All Kinds of Sicknesses

I discovered there was nothing Jesus didn't heal.

> He healed *all kinds of sicknesses* and diseases. (Matt. 8:13, emphasis mine)

> Then the great multitudes came to Him, having with them the lame, blind, mute, maimed, and many others; and they laid them down at Jesus feet and He healed them. (Matt. 15:30)

The Word

These are all really great stories. And I was having fun seeing what Jesus did, but I was still uncertain. *Do I believe the types of healings I'm reading about are still for today?* The Bible says Jesus Christ is the same yesterday, today, and forever (Heb. 13:8), but Jesus is not physically here. This seemed to make sense, and then it was confusing at the same time.

I continued searching, asking questions. *I want to know.* After several months, my faith started to increase. I began seeing I was called to be the hands and feet of Jesus. I also began to see that everyone who believes in Jesus has received authority to lay hands on the sick and to see the power of Jesus heal people.

Jesus said we would see greater works than what He did after He died and rose.

> Most assuredly, I say to you, he who believes in Me, the works that I do he will do also; and greater works than these he will do, because I go to the Father. (John 14:12)

I'm changing. I'm beginning to believe things I haven't believed before. I believe what I'm reading in the Bible can happen today. I did believe these things, but I also found myself saying, "I only want to see what God is doing and not something weird." I've seen some strange things before, and I don't want to be a part of something fake. I only want to be a part of what Jesus is doing. I know that God is taking me somewhere new because it's His Word that has changed me.

Then it happened.

About one year later, I was walking through the house, and I reached the same spot where I'd heard the voice back in January of 2005, the voice that said, "It's going to be a really bad year." Except this time, as I walked in that same spot, I almost dropped to my knees with a knowing in my heart like I'd never known before. It was a knowing that I know—that I know—*that I know*—God is going to heal Paige!

I can't explain it any other way than to say, "I just know!" It's not because she needs it or I need it, because she's perfect the way she is. What God said about her when she was born is still true. She's perfect. He didn't change His mind. The healing is going to take place because God is God, and God heals. He's supernatural, yet it's natural for Him. He does things we can't see. It's called faith. He's going to heal Paige so He will be glorified. There's no way any medical doctor can heal Paige the way God can. The healing would cause others to want to know more about this God that healed Paige. I became filled with a joy that no one can take away from me. My eyes glistened with tears just thinking about God's goodness in my life.

> Blessed is she who believed, for there will be a fulfillment of those things which were told her from the Lord. (Luke 1:45)

I could hardly wait to share this news! The first three people I shared this news with all had different responses:

The first response from a friend was happy.

The second response from a family member was excited.

The third response came from another friend who listened to what I said, but they were probably thinking, *She's not thinking straight.*

It's okay. I didn't care what people thought. I knew what I'd heard, and what I'd heard wasn't anything I'd been asking for. It wasn't my idea. I knew what I'd heard hadn't come from me—it came from God, and it brought me fullness of joy!

Paige

After a brief time, my thoughts turned toward Paige. *If God is going to do this for Paige then I need to let her know about it.* Before I had a chance to act on this though, God gave me a dream. In this dream, I saw Paige healed. Until now, I'd never had a dream like this. I'd never seen Paige healed.

The Dream

I was watching a little girl in a wheelchair. At first, I didn't recognize her. Then as I stood there watching, I saw the wheelchair begin to morph into something different. It was transforming from a wheelchair to a bicycle. This little girl was now riding a bicycle, and she was riding it fast. She was laughing and smiling, and it was obvious she was very happy. She rode around a large tree and then dropped the bicycle onto the ground. She jumped off the bicycle and started running around a tree.

I didn't recognize her until the moment she jumped off the bicycle. That's when I realized it was Paige! Paige's wheelchair had morphed into a bicycle, and Paige was riding the bicycle. She was the one who'd jumped off the bicycle, and she was filled with joy as she ran around this big tree. As soon as it registered in my mind what was happening, I started calling people who were nearby to find out if they'd seen what had happened. The people there were various members of our family, and they had seen it too!

Paige was completely healed. She was still petite, but taller than she is today. She was filled with contagious joy!

I believed this dream was the perfect way for me to share with Paige what God had revealed to me about healing her, so I told her about it.

"Paige, I saw you riding a bicycle. I saw you get off of the bicycle, and you were running."

She listened, not saying a word.

"God is going to heal you so you can ride a bicycle and walk without a walker."

As I was saying those words, I thought, *These are pretty big and bold statements for me to be telling Paige. I sure don't want to mislead her and speak things that may never happen. That doesn't feel very loving.* But I chose to put my trust in God because He is a loving God.

Paige being Paige accepted everything I said. She repeated back to me that God was going to heal her so she could ride a bicycle and walk without a walker. She understood everything I said. Her childlike faith believed in those things that had taken me months to comprehend.

Then I had a second dream. This dream was about Paige and one of the doctors she was currently seeing. She was at his office and functioning at a very high level. He was astounded at what he was seeing. Her verbal skills, her humor, her conversation—all were like nothing he had seen before.

Until I heard God speak to me about Paige's healing, I'd never had dreams about her being healed before. Now, within a very short time, I'd had two dreams.

And then I had a third dream.

Paige was in the back of what resembled a white truck. There were a lot of other people in the truck with her. There was a lot going on, which I felt represented being pulled in many different directions. In the dream, I heard God remind me not to lose sight of Paige's healing. He said, "Even though a lot is going on, she is still being healed. Notice what I'm doing. Her complete healing and instant miracle are still taking place. She is being healed now and will still be healed through a visible miracle in her body."

God was definitely speaking to me about healing Paige's entire body, first as I was walking through the house and now in my dreams.

He was reminding me that this was His idea, and He didn't want me to lose sight of what He was doing.

Things continued happening for me. During worship one night, I sensed an overwhelming move of the Holy Spirit within me. I felt like I could cry as I heard God say, "Paige is going to be healed by Me and Me alone. She's going to respond to My touch and the atmosphere. It's not going to be when someone is praying for her."

I was hearing God more clearly and more often than ever before. I'd asked for this because I wanted to have a relationship with a true and living God, and He'd now become alive in my life.

I wanted this for Paige! *I'm putting my trust in God, but how can I help Paige trust God? How can I show her that God is real and she can trust Him too?*

Before now, Paige had never been able to get into bed by herself. I'm not sure if she needed more strength or coordination, or if her bed was just too high to get into (given her small stature). Since I was looking for an opportunity to show her that God is real, I had an idea. Paige and I were going to ask God to help her get into bed, and I wasn't going to help.

That evening when Paige was ready for bed, I said, "God is going to help you get into bed tonight." I wasn't sure if she understood what I meant, but I stepped back and waited to see what would happen.

With one hand on the headboard and one foot on the foot rail, Paige pushed herself off of the floor to gain the needed momentum to pull herself up and get into bed. As she was pulling herself up, I didn't move. I just watched. I watched to see what God was going to do. She didn't make it. She came right back down onto the floor. So I said again, "God's going to help you. God's going to help you get into bed." Then I prayed, stepping out in faith and trusting God to move.

Paige tried again and again while I watched without jumping in to help her. Paige finally fell into bed, and as she landed on the pillow, her face lit up with a great big smile. She was so delighted. I marveled when I heard her give thanks to God.

She said, "Thank You, God, for helping Paige get into bed."

God had helped Paige! He helped her get into bed. I believe this is when Paige began knowing about a God who could help her, a God she could trust.

Paige began to change. In the past when I'd asked her if she needed help, sometimes she'd say yes and sometimes she'd say no. But after God helped her into bed, she'd say, "No, God's helping Paige." And He was.

Paige and God began having a different kind of relationship with each other. He became more real to her. Not only did she ask Him to help her but she also began to speak about Him often. She'd often say, "Go, God!" "Come on, God," "Yay, God!" "I want God to come over," or "I want to pray to God."

Although she couldn't read the Bible, I'd see her with her Bible in her lap, flipping through the pages. Every once in a while, I'd see her put a mark on a page or highlight something.

Paige is so observant. She doesn't miss anything, and she has a great memory. She'd seen people get baptized at our church, so she was able to communicate when she wanted to be baptized. I hadn't seen anyone with special needs baptized before, but I trusted God would make a way for it to happen. So I contacted the church, and God did make a way.

On November 15, 2009, when Paige was eighteen, I had the honor and privilege of carrying her into the baptismal. Together we went up some stairs and then down some stairs into the water. As family and friends watched, the pastor asked Paige if she accepted Jesus into her heart. After she said yes, Paige was baptized in the Name of the Father and of the Son and of the Holy Spirit!

Jesus was now living life with Paige!

Cool Name

Behold, the former things have come to pass, and new things I declare; before they spring forth, I tell you of them.
Isaiah 42:9

I KNEW WITHOUT A DOUBT I'd marry again. And I also knew I would take this person's last name. But although I knew I'd do this, God was the only one who knew I had some feelings about it.

During one of my quiet times, I began talking with God about it. "God, I know that when I get married again, I'm going to take this man's last name. You'd think I'd be excited about this, but I'm not. I know in that moment of union my last name will become different than Paige's last name. And just thinking about this brings sadness to my heart."

To others, this may not seem important. But to me, there was something about being separated from Paige in this way that caused me to feel sad. I anticipated that it was going to feel like another loss in my life. In some way, I felt like although I'd been the one who had stood by Paige and cared for her, she and her dad would still share the same last name but not me.

I searched my heart. *Have I truly forgiven him?* Yes, I had. But I still knew I was going to have to walk through another consequence of divorce. I tucked away this conversation with God in my memory and in my journal. Only God and I knew.

In May of 2009, my heart began stirring. What I mean is I started having the desire to be married again. Since being divorced, I'd had none of those feelings stirred up. I'd been completely content just hanging out with God. Solomon 2:7 refers to this stirring: "Do not stir up or awaken love until it pleases." I knew this stirring was an indication that God was about to take me into a new season—one of courtship.

I'm getting married again, and it's going to be soon.

God had established Paige and me on a specific journey. He'd already confirmed to me He was going to heal Paige. He'd confirmed that she would receive a miracle of healing in her body—a creative miracle! It was God who had brought me to this place of faith, yet I couldn't imagine this person who would be able to come beside us on this journey. I was so certain of God's *declaration* that I was willing to sacrifice marriage to continue stewarding Paige's life in the direction I felt God was taking us.

> When He, the Spirit of truth, has come, He will guide you into all truth; for He will not speak on His own authority, but whatever He hears He will speak; and He will tell you things to come. He will glorify Me, for He will take of what is Mine and declare it to you. (John 16: 13–14)

My desire was to date *only* the person God had for me to date. I didn't want to go on a date "just to be dating." Christ had established my identity in Him and not in being married. My desire was to mirror God's image on the earth. My prayer was to be protected and for no one to be able to approach me except "the only one" God had for me. As I walked into this next season, my eyes were open to see what God wanted me to see, and my ears were listening to hear what He wanted me to hear.

Four months later, I was sitting at a coffee shop with some friends from church when my eyes landed on someone new. Filled with curiosity, I kept looking at him. *Who is he? Where did he come from? I don't remember seeing him before.* But he was with a group of people I'd met with off and on for several months. There were no introductions that evening, just awareness and curiosity.

Shortly after the coffee shop experience, I saw him again at another gathering. This time I was keenly aware he was able to approach me and engage me in conversation. I was guarded and kept the wall up around my heart, but I was curious about what was going on.

A couple of weeks later, I received a friend request on Facebook, but I wasn't sure I knew the person. Whoever it was, they'd made a comment, "Cool name!"

"Cool name?" Who is this person? What do they mean by "cool name"?

As I took a closer look at the profile photo, it registered. *It's that guy! It's that man I've been talking with—the man who was able to approach me. But I still don't understand what he means by "cool name."* And then I saw it. As I read his first and last name, I finally understood. I stared at it, a bit shocked and surprised—his last name was the same last name as mine!

My head immediately flooded with all kinds of thoughts. *God, is this the one? He has the same last name as me!* As crazy as it sounds, I did think, *Am I going to marry this man?* I continued talking with God. "You know this is one of the deepest longings in my heart, to have the same last name as Paige. But I don't even know who this man is. What are You doing here, God?"

Of course, God knew what He was doing. This is what He used to get me to take a second look at this man. There were other things that kept me looking, but it was the last name that got my full attention, the thing that moved me beyond just curiosity. It was this "suddenly" that God did that caused me to trust Him with the journey He was taking me on—the journey of courtship with my soon-to-be husband.

Tommy was the name of the man I'd met. Before the Facebook friend request, this was all I'd known. I accepted the friend request, and as many people do, I looked through all of his photos, his friends, and his timeline.

I have a lot of questions, God. I need to know a lot more about this man.

Although I didn't know Tommy, I sensed I was supposed to be open to getting to know him. It was obvious he knew we shared the same last name. I wanted to know if he saw this spiritually as I did. I wanted to know where he was with his faith. I wanted to know what he knew about being a spiritual leader in the home. I needed to know where he was in his beliefs about healing. It seemed like I had a lot of questions for God to answer.

God being God, He began giving me the answers I was looking for. The next time I saw Tommy, he mentioned without asking that he'd received a healing in his body. He shared how it had happened, where he was at the time, and how God had healed him.

He then went on to share his thoughts about being the spiritual leader in the home. *I can't believe this. God is giving me the answers to some of the things I want to know. I haven't even asked Tommy these questions, yet these answers are just coming my way! It's as if God is showing me He heard me when I asked Him all of my questions.* I was encouraged by this, and it brought me great peace.

Although I was gathering information about Tommy, I realized there were many things he didn't know about me. Most significantly, I knew he needed to know more about Paige and me—our story—our journey, the journey God had us on.

I wrote in my journal: "It's important for me to be able to share You, Lord, what You are saying to me about Paige. How will Tommy feel about this? I know that what I share with him is going to be very important for this relationship. I believe I will know more, depending on how he responds. I may be disappointed. What I do know, is that I trust You God."

Although I knew how important this was, I waited to share this information. God continued to confirm in more ways that Tommy was the one He had for me and Paige. I trusted God with every aspect of this process. Although we had months and months of conversations, I had known within three weeks of meeting Tommy that he would be my husband.

I even took a bold step of faith and wrote it in my journal: "Okay, Lord, I'm going to write down what I believe You are saying to me: I believe Tommy is the one I will marry. I believe we will marry in 2010."

When I wrote those words in faith, he and I had not been on one date. We were both "gathering information" about each other. Although I was attracted to him, I was first attracted to his heart. *I see a good man. I see a man seeking after God. I see a man who wants to be in a marriage God's way. I see a man who loves his family. I see a spiritual leader. I see a man who believes in healing.* God showed me all these things.

After three months of conversations, I felt prompted to give Tommy a set of CDs about running a business God's way. One of the CDs speaks about going on sabbaticals. Tommy had never been on a sabbatical before, and after listening to the CDs, he decided he wanted to go on one. What I didn't know was that he went on this sabbatical to seek God about me.

Tommy had been having conversations with God about me, and he had kept hearing, "You can't date Sharon." He hadn't understood this, so in January 2010 when he went on his first sabbatical, he asked God about our relationship. During that period of three days of talking with God, Tommy got "approval" to move forward. God also spoke to Tommy about Paige.

In addition to keeping the same last name as Paige, I had another desire in my heart. To some it might seem strange, but it was important to me. Besides God, I let one of my friends in on this desire, a friend named Linda who God brought into my life during what I affectionately refer to as "my season of singleness." I needed a good friend during this season and we were so much alike.

One evening we were enjoying a nice dinner and good conversation. We both knew we'd get married again, and that night we were dreaming about our futures. We laughed about many things—things we'd been through, things we'd done, things we thought about. We laughed a lot. Then the atmosphere changed, and we began sharing heart to heart. Each of us shared qualities we'd like to have in a husband.

I shared one of my desires with Linda. "I know this may sound strange, but it's going to be important for this man to put Paige's chair in the car for me. I'm not sure why this is so significant to me, but it does matter. There's something about this gesture that would be heartwarming. It feels caring. It feels right." *Yes, it's important to me.*

As soon as I saw Tommy after his sabbatical, I knew something was different. *Something's changed. It isn't just the rose in his hand—he's different!* He was eager to share what God had spoken to him, and I was just as eager to hear, so we sat in a quiet booth at a local restaurant. When Tommy began sharing, I quickly learned God had given him permission to pursue me through courtship!

If courtship wasn't enough, a week or so later Tommy said, "I want to share something else I heard on sabbatical."

He had my attention; my ears positioned to hear.

"God spoke to me about Paige."

That's nice. "What did He say?"

"God talked to me about Paige's chair."

My heart awakened in utter amazement at those words.

"I would like to put Paige's chair in the car for you."

Stunned, I couldn't believe what I was hearing. *Really? Are you kidding me?* I didn't say those words out loud, but I felt awestruck and truly astonished at what I'd just heard. It was as if God was revealing my thoughts and desires to Tommy. *God is speaking to him about me. And not only me but about me and Paige.*

It felt like God was saying to me, "Look what I'm doing here for you, Sharon. I care deeply for you. You can trust me. I even care for the deepest longings in your heart."

Delight yourself also in the Lord,
And He shall give you the desires of your heart. (Ps. 37:4)

On this same sabbatical, Tommy had heard from God that he was supposed to serve in healing ministry with me. When I heard this, I remembered the prophetic word I'd received almost two years ago from my new friend Kim at the church picnic—the words regarding my future husband: "You will marry again. This man is going to be very strong in his faith. This man that you marry will be instrumental in the healing of your daughter."

I still hadn't had a conversation with Tommy about what God was doing in Paige's and my life, but it was obvious to me that God was speaking to Tommy for me. Still not saying a word, I continued to trust God in this process. Everything I was experiencing, all the confirmations, was causing me to believe that God had brought someone special into my life—someone aligned with the purposes and plans He'd already spoken to me about my life with Paige.

What I had written in my journal about being married in 2010 came to pass. Tommy and I married nine months later, to the day, after we met. We married and became a blended family. Tommy has four adult children, and I have Paige. We became a family of seven.

A family "made in heaven."

Blended Family

Saying "I do" doesn't automatically mean "happily ever after." Blending a family takes work. It takes a conscious effort not only to work on your marriage but also to take everyone else's feelings into account. Tommy and I found out soon enough we couldn't just "hang out" and talk for hours. We had other eyes watching and wondering what was going on. Everyone wanted to know how they fit into this family now, and Paige was one of them.

Since the divorce, Paige had had my undivided attention. Now I was sharing my time with her, and she could see something had changed because it had. I'm not sure how well she was able to comprehend what had taken place—that Tommy and I married—because she wasn't able to communicate the fullness of her thoughts with me. Was she wondering, *Who is this person living in our home? Who is this Tommy? And what happened to my mom?*

Although Paige couldn't communicate what was going on inside of her, there was definitely a change in her demeanor. She was quiet. She was in deep thought. She was thinking about something. Tommy and I recognized this change, and we both knew we needed to prioritize her needs and desires as well. Right then, she needed us to help steward this change in her life.

God's order needs to be established. In blended families, God's original design is out of order. God's original design is for husband and wife to become one before the children. We knew it would be important for Paige to see that Tommy and Mom come first. Trusting in God, and in this order, we believed our love for each other and the security of our relationship would bring her security.

Tommy and I made some adjustments. When Tommy came home from work, we greeted each other first so she could see the order, but instead of the two of us catching up, we limited our conversation to a brief greeting of a few minutes. Then we would talk with Paige to see how she was doing, and we'd ask her questions about her day. We all three shared in this time. Once her love tank was full, Tommy and I connected again.

I began feeling like I was the one who needed to help bridge the gap between Tommy and Paige. In order for this to happen, I knew I needed to step back and allow Tommy to enter into her life, to become a part of her life, and to do things I normally did for her. I chose to step back because I loved her and I was secure in my relationship with her. I knew my place as Mom in her life, and I knew it was good for her to have other people in her life who loved and cared for her besides me.

I stepped back out of the primary caregiver role and focus of Paige's life so Tommy and Paige could develop a closer relationship. Paige being Paige, and Tommy being Tommy, it didn't take long for the two of them to connect deeply.

Paige began to realize our relationship had not changed. Mom was still here. She also became secure in Mom's relationship with Tommy. She saw it was good, and in the end, she basically just needed reassurance that she hadn't lost anything. Instead, something had been added. She now had Tommy, her bonus dad.

If you're reading this, and you're a single mom of a child with special needs, I want to encourage you. I've had some moms say to me, "I don't know if anyone will want to marry me since I have a child with special needs." I'd like to share with you that I never once had those thoughts. I never doubted I would marry again. I never doubted someone would be able to love both Paige and me. I always knew we were a "package deal" because whoever came along would be marrying me and Paige. I also knew that whoever I married would be blessed by the two of us. I didn't see any of this as prideful or arrogant. I just knew we were both very loveable and loving. I never believed there was anything "wrong" or "different" about us. We were and are easy to love.

As a man thinks in his heart, so is he. (Prov. 23:7)

God loves you. He loves your child. He desires for you to have good things, and He wants to fulfill the desires of your heart because He put them there. As you look to Him, He will guide you, and He will lead you so you can walk into His promises over your life. It is a process, but He is faithful!

One year later, Tommy had two dreams right in a row about Paige. Those dreams seemed very significant to both of us. Like me, Tommy was having dreams about Paige being healed.

Tommy's first dream:

"Sharon and I were with Paige at an event. As we were leaving, I noticed that Paige wasn't in her chair—she was crawling behind it. Sharon and I were pushing her chair in front of her. She was able to keep up by crawling. Then I found myself standing back, watching Paige follow Sharon as she began to walk without a walker. Sharon began to run, and Paige kept up by walking very fast. She was still bent over, but she was walking without a walker.

"*I've never seen Paige do that before. God is healing Paige!* Then I found myself in front of Paige, about twenty feet or so. I called to her, and she came running over to me. She was standing right in front of me, and I said to her, 'Paige, do you know that God is healing you right now?' As I was saying these words I began to weep, and as I wept, she changed right before my eyes. Her facial features changed, and she stood up and grew taller, maybe about six inches shorter than her mom. She just stood there with a big smile, her eyes closed, her hands by her sides with her palms facing me, as if she were saying, 'Look at me!'"

Tommy's second dream:

"We were at a gathering, I'm not sure where, but I asked Paige a question, and she answered me with a word I had not heard her use before. Then she started stringing words together that I had not heard before. Then she strung sentences together, and her speech cleared up, and she began to talk normally, using long sentences."

To us, these dreams are continued confirmation of God's promise to heal Paige. But now, God was speaking beyond me. He was now speaking to my husband, Paige's bonus dad.

Tommy was now living life with Paige.

Legacy

> *Grant to Your servants that with all boldness they may speak Your word, by stretching out Your hand to heal, and that signs and wonders may be done through the name of Your holy servant.*
> Acts 4:29–30

I HEARD THE LANDING GEAR releasing, which meant only one thing to me—we were about to land. Filled with curiosity, I looked out the window. *Mountains?* I couldn't believe there were mountains. It's as if I were seeing mountains for the first time in my life. They are breathtaking—so green, so lush, so full of life! These mountains seemed to have more meaning to me than all the other mountains I've ever seen. I looked at them intently, not wanting to miss one of them, trying to capture those few moments in my mind so I could remember them forever. My heart swelled with unidentified emotions, and my eyes began filling with tears. These tears weren't either happy or sad, but I knew they had a significant meaning.

I was coming back to Guadalajara, Mexico, the place where I had been born. Although I was adopted, I never had any overwhelming desire to search out my birth parents, but I have wondered about the place where I was born. The country. The people. The part of me that came from there.

This was a planned trip, but there wasn't any way to know ahead of time what I might experience or how I'd be filled with this unexpected delight. After landing and receiving the clearance to exit, I gathered my things and began to walk off the airplane. One foot, then the other—then I stepped onto this unfamiliar soil. It's as if I had walked out of a time capsule. Life had been going on here, but I had been living life somewhere else. In the moment my feet stepped back into this place, I was suddenly filled with overwhelming joy.

Everything seemed so vibrant and new. Just like the mountains, it was as if I were seeing things I'd never seen before. The truth is, I had never seen them. I was only one day old when my parents came to get me. They knew about the timing of my birth from missionaries living in the area. When it was time, they had traveled to Guadalajara to get me and bring me back to the United States. I'd only been on this soil for a few days before leaving for the US. Now after more than fifty years, I was back.

Walking through customs, I showed the man at the counter my passport. "I was born here!"

He seemed interested enough, so I continued. "I'm adopted! This is the first time I've been back in over fifty years."

Sharing my story didn't stop with him though. I was like a kid in a candy store! I told my story to anyone and everyone who would listen.

I was not here on vacation but on a ministry trip, a trip that presented itself only a few months ago. I was searching the internet when I discovered this trip with Wheels for the World.

Wheels for the World (WFTW) is an organization that delivers wheelchairs and walkers to the disabled in other countries where they don't have access to things like we do in the United States. I've traveled with WFTW before, but until now I'd never seen a trip to

Guadalajara on their website. My eyes lit up when I saw it. *I can't wait to share this with Tommy!* I located him in the other room.

"I've found our next mission trip. Can you guess where it is?"

Without skipping a beat, he said, "Guadalajara." It was his first guess.

I stood there in utter amazement, then squealed with excitement because I knew we were both in unity. This unity only confirmed that we were supposed to take this trip. Moving forward in agreement, we each filled out the application to become part of the team. Tommy was going to be a mechanic, making modifications to the wheelchairs, and I was going to be his assistant.

Now we were here in Guadalajara.

Even as we loaded into the van, I kept looking around, taking in all the sights and sounds of the city. Much larger than I'd imagined, Guadalajara was a big city, similar to the area where we lived. *I know I was born here, but where?* I didn't have any knowledge of the exact location. But there was an address on my birth certificate where I was registered in Guadalajara, the address where my parents had stayed when they came to get me.

Throughout the drive to the hotel, I wondered where the address was. *Are we driving by it right now? Are we anywhere close to it?* In seeing the magnitude of this city, I began to realize, *I may never know where this address is. We're not here on vacation or for personal reasons—we're here as part of a ministry team. We're on their schedule, and we're here to serve the people of Guadalajara.*

Two days into the trip, the excitement hadn't diminished. I was having the time of my life serving the people of Guadalajara. Then our van driver came up to me and asked for the address on my birth certificate. Not thinking much about it, I gave it to him. *At least I'll know where it is.*

In a few moments, he returned with an interpreter who informed me that the address was four blocks from the church where we were serving! *What? Four blocks! You've got to be kidding!* I couldn't believe what I was hearing. *This city has over a million people in it, and I'm only four blocks from where my parents stayed when they came to get me. What are the odds of that? God is definitely up to something here. How in the world did I get within four blocks of where my parents stayed when I was born?*

Since the entire team had heard my story, they were almost as excited as I was when they found out how close we were. I waited patiently to see what would happen next. *Will I be able to go to this address?*

The team leaders made certain we did, and during the next break in the schedule, several of us walked the four blocks. We didn't get every step recorded on video, but I did record every step in my memory. And with each step, I knew I was getting closer and my anticipation grew. I was going to a place I hadn't been since I was a baby.

Using current technology, we finally reached the "red dot" on the cell phone. We had arrived—we'd found the address on my birth certificate. I looked up, and in front of me stood a two-story building painted white and teal. I was now standing in front of the building I was inside of over fifty years ago. In a sense, I was "back home," but it had never been my home.

Suddenly, I was caught by surprise. It was as if my spirit knew I'd been here before, because my emotions took over, leaving me in sheer disbelief at the goodness of my life. I just wanted to tell my birth parents "Thank you"—to thank them for giving me such a good life, especially my birth mom. I wanted her to know she had made the right decision. In those moments, I experienced overwhelming thankfulness and gratitude for the parents who had chosen me, the ones who had sought me out and had given me such a good life. *I'm just so thankful that this was the plan God had for me.* Tears of joy rolled down my face.

I could've gone back home right then and been completely satisfied with the trip, yet we still had five or more days to go. Tommy was in his element, making adjustments and modifications to the wheelchairs. He's very mechanically inclined and can make almost anything work, and it brings him great joy when he can be a part of making others happy.

I was in my element as well. Although I had signed up as Tommy's assistant, I found myself in conversations with the moms of children with special needs. With a translator, I was able to communicate, mom to mom, heart to heart with them, and when they heard about my daughter with special needs, there was an immediate connection. I showed them pictures of Paige. It was also meaningful for them to know I was born here. Encouraging and praying for them brought me great joy.

I'm not sure what you're doing here, God, but I know something's up. Not only am I back where I was born, I'm within four blocks of where my parents stayed when they came to get me. I have a daughter with special needs, and I'm serving families of children with special needs. I'm here with the man You brought into my life, and he loves being here. God was definitely doing something on this trip.

At the end of the week, Tommy and I boarded the airplane to return home. Both of us felt a sense of accomplishment, and our hearts were grateful for our time here. I was pleased I had the opportunity to come back to the place of my birth and serve the people of Guadalajara. I satisfied my curiosity, and I didn't need to go back.

A year passed. Then unexpectedly, we received a phone call from the team leaders with Wheels for the World.

"We're calling to see if you two will be coming back this year."

I never expected to get this call. I hadn't planned to go back, and I wasn't sure if I wanted to go back. I had such great memories of our time there, I didn't want anything to spoil it.

We were moving that year, so it seemed like a logical reason not to go.

"Thank you so much for calling and thinking of us," I said, "but we're moving this year and don't think it's a good idea for us to go." We knew they'd hoped for a different answer, but they were very gracious and accepted it.

One year later, my cell phone rang, and I could see it was one of the team leaders from Wheels for the World. Tommy waited nearby as I answered the phone. The wife with her husband were on the other line. All four of us shared what had been going on in our lives. I kept thinking, *I have no intentions of returning to Guadalajara. I hope they don't ask.* But they did.

"Will you and Tommy be joining us in Guadalajara this year?"

I don't know if I want to go, God. How do we answer this question? I felt torn. *Paige!* The last time we were in Guadalajara, I'd wondered if we would ever bring her there.

Just like I'd grown in my relationship with God, Paige had grown as well. She now carries an anointing of the presence of God on her life and has a ministry of her own. A very noticeable intensity rises up inside her, and when this happens, she tells us she wants to pray for people. She loves to pray for others.

Sometimes she wants to pray for something very specific, like a person's heart, arm, or leg. When approached, everyone usually agrees to let Paige pray for them. Most people aren't seeking prayer, but they politely say yes more than likely just to be nice. Over and over again, many people are caught off guard at how the encounter with Paige impacts them.

I've watched Paige lay hands on people and see their eyes fill with tears. Sometimes you can understand what she's saying, and other times you can barely hear her. She may speak a series of sentences or just a few words. Somehow, whether they can hear or understand the words she's speaking, it really doesn't matter. What matters is what God does through the laying on of hands and Paige's obedience to respond to what's going on inside her heart. The impact has been significant. Many have come back and told us that when Paige prayed for them, they've been healed.

With the Guadalajara team leaders still on the other end of the line and Tommy nearby, I replied, "If we do go back to Guadalajara, I feel like Paige is supposed to go with us." They asked me for more information, so I told them about Paige—who she is, her life, and why I felt like she was supposed to go. The team leaders listened to what I had to say and then told us they would need to get approval from the organization for Paige to go. We understood. I had expressed what was in my heart and trusted God with the rest.

A few months later, my cell phone rang, and it was one of the team leaders with Wheels for the World. I barely said hello before I heard, "Sharon! We've got great news! Paige has been accepted to go to Guadalajara!" I chuckled silently and shook my head in disbelief. *I can't believe what I'm hearing.* Quickly though, joy filled me, and there was laughter in my heart. God had a sense of humor, and I knew what He was saying.

We're going back to Guadalajara! God has opened a door for Paige to go to Guadalajara! I don't have to think about it anymore—I know. I know what the answer's going to be. When the question came, "Will you go?" I said, "Yes! Yes! We're all going!"

After hanging up the phone, I stood there still shaking my head in disbelief. *I can't believe I'm going back to Guadalajara! And this time I'm going back with Paige.*

We knew Paige enjoyed traveling and that she had a heart to pray for people, but she didn't know what we'd just signed her up to do. Tommy and I talked with her together about this trip.

"Paige!" I said. "Tommy and I have something to tell you."

She was attentive.

"We're going on a mission trip! We're going to Guadalajara, Mexico!"

Big word. She was processing what I'd just said.

"We're going to go pray for people in wheelchairs."

This got her attention, and Paige began to repeat the words mission trip and Mexico, and she made an attempt at saying Guadalajara. Although she may not have comprehended everything she'd just heard, she was all in!

She knew it had to do with traveling on an airplane, which she loved. She knew it had to do with wheelchairs, which she was familiar with, as she'd had one of her own. She knew she'd be praying, which she was comfortable with. Although she didn't understand everything about this trip, we didn't either, but we did know Paige was supposed to go.

The day we traveled back to Guadalajara was quite surreal for me. *Tommy, Sharon, and Paige are headed to Guadalajara! My birthplace. I'm going back to a place I truly had no plans to return to. I don't know what this is all about, God, but I'm open to what You're doing here.*

After a quick flight, we landed. It'd been two years, but we were back. *I'm not sure how it's going to feel getting off the airplane and revisiting the places I saw last time—the places that felt kind of "magical" seeing them for the first time.* Strangely enough, as I stepped off the airplane, everything felt all new again. Paige was here.

The other team members met us at the airport. They knew Tommy and me, but they hadn't met Paige. They saw us pushing Paige in a chair, and later they saw her walk with a walker. And they soon found out that she was verbal, even though they didn't understand many of the words she was speaking. Outwardly they saw a disability, but it didn't take long for them to move beyond this and see the joy she carried—the anointing of courage and encouragement upon her—and to experience her contagious laugh! They saw her humor as we helped translate what she was saying. Paige is very relational, and soon enough everyone had their own connection with her.

Being a team member meant we each had a job assignment. On paper, the various job assignments didn't quite fit Paige. The trip roster had her listed as administration, and at first I wasn't sure how she was going to make a contribution.

Then we saw the bracelets!

These are gospel bracelets the team brought with them, and they asked us to hand them out to the wheelchair recipients. We put Paige in charge of handing them out.

I handed her the bag of bracelets and suggested she give them to the children as they received their wheelchairs. This was something she was easily able to do, and she liked it. Knowing how much Paige liked to pray, I also suggested she pray for the children. She was able to do that, and she liked it too. It didn't take her long to get into the rhythm of this job assignment.

In fact, she was enjoying doing these things so much that we began looking for more opportunities. She started handing out the bracelets and praying for everyone she could find who was being fitted for a wheelchair or a walker. That's how we discovered Paige's job assignment of evangelism. She was in her element. She was giving because she loves to give. And she was praying for people because she loves to pray! Whether the recipient was old or young didn't matter, Paige prayed. People watched. Paige witnessed. Paige moved on people's hearts. Paige brought hope and love to the people in Guadalajara, Mexico.

At the end of the week, we headed back to the airport. This had been an amazing mission trip. And it hadn't diminished my memories from two years earlier either. They were still there, only now I had new memories, memories of Paige on her first mission trip.

As we were boarding the airplane, one of the team leaders came up to our family and said, "It was so great having Paige with us this year. She added another dimension to the team."

I treasured those words in my heart. I was so proud of Paige.

Then she said, "We'd love for her to come back again next year."

I chuckled inside. Paige had just been asked to come back to Guadalajara!

Here we go again. God, You really do have a sense of humor. Not only did You open a door for Paige to go to Guadalajara, but You made a way for her to come back again.

What I've discovered is that God is a God of suddenly. Many times I've had a plan for my life, and then suddenly, out of nowhere, I'm going in a completely different direction. Although these sudden changes initially catch me off guard, when I stop and take a moment to see what's really going on, I often realize that God's hand is in the middle of it. When I realize that, it's easier for me to come into alignment, or agreement, with what's taking place because I know He's doing it. I can trust Him. I wasn't planning on returning to Guadalajara, but God had different plans for our family. He wanted Paige to go.

I also know God opens doors and shuts doors. When doors open, they are doors of opportunity. Doors of opportunity can be exciting to walk through when you know they're part of God's plan for your life. His plans are much better than our plans. God opened a door for Paige to go on an international mission trip, and we walked through it. Although not fully understanding, we came into agreement with God's plans for us.

> For as the heavens are higher than the earth,
> So, are My ways higher than your ways,
> And My thoughts than your thoughts. (Isa. 55:9)

As we journey and co-labor with God, there is an ebb and flow throughout our lives. During this journey with Paige, my desire has always been to steward her life in the direction that God is taking her. I know His plans for her are greater than any plan of mine. And because of this, my eyes are always looking to see, my ears are always listening to hear, and my heart is always desiring to trust, because I know God loves Paige more than I do. He's just blessed me to be the person who gets to steward her life, for His glory.

I'm blessed to be living life with Paige.

The Greatest Gift

> *And though I have the gift of prophecy, and understand all mysteries and all knowledge, and though I have all faith, so that I could remove mountains, but have not love, I am nothing.*
> 1 Corinthians 13:2

AS I SIT IN a local coffee shop today, I'm surrounded by people involved in various conversations or working on their laptops. All of this activity around me makes it almost too hard to focus, but then I begin to hear music playing in the background. It's not very loud, so I could've missed it. Yet for some reason it has my attention. I lean in so I can hear the words better. And as I listen, something begins to happen inside me. This song—the words, the melody—is touching the deep places of my heart. There's an intensity about their meaning that causes me to wipe my eyes.

It's a familiar song. I've heard these words before. *Why are these words affecting me like this today?* I've known this song as a love song between a man and a woman, but right now it feels more like my love song between Paige and me. I feel like God is using these words to talk with me about my life with Paige.

I keep hearing the words, "How deep is your love?"

It's as if God is saying to me, "How deep is your love for Paige? I really need to know."

"How deep is your love for your daughter with the big brown eyes? I really need to know."

"How deep is your love for this person I've entrusted into your care? I really need to know."

"How deep is your love for this person I chose for you to love?—to love her like I do? I really need to know."

"How deep is your love for the gift, the blessing, I've given to you? I really need to know."

My answer is, "My love is deep!" It's always been deep. Have I always recognized it as being a deep love? Probably not. I've just known that I love her. Right now, through this song, God is showing me that my love for Paige has always been deep. From the moment she was born, He's been asking me, "How deep is your love?" He's wanted to see, and He's wanted to know.

I'm not perfect, and I haven't always done it right with Paige, but my heart's desire has always been to love her deeply. I've always wanted Paige to have no doubt that I love her—for her to feel "special." I've always loved her from a deep place within my heart.

Although the song I'm listening to is a love song written by the Bee Gees, God has a love song in His Word, the Bible. It's in 1 Corinthians 13:4–7 (NIV):

> Love is patient, love is kind. It does not envy, it does not boast, it is not proud. It does not dishonor others, it is not self-seeking, it is not easily angered, it keeps no record of wrongs. Love does not delight in evil, but rejoices with the truth. It always protects, always trusts, always hopes, always perseveres.

Love is patient. Before Paige was born, I thought I was fairly patient. However, she's taught me to be more patient. Our world seems to be in such a hurry, but Paige's world is a bit slower.

She's quite slow and methodical. She needs extra time for almost everything. It takes her extra time to get dressed. It takes her longer to eat than everyone else at the table. She walks with a walker at a very steady pace, but she's never in a hurry. Love is patient.

Love is kind. When Paige was born, it seemed as if she was born into a world that was so unkind to her. A cold and unloving world. I wanted her to experience a life that isn't harsh and unkind. I was tender and gentle with her, creating an atmosphere of trust. Desiring her brain and body to heal, I created an atmosphere of peace. I spoke words of affirmation and life over her, creating an atmosphere of hope. I've given her big long hugs, conveying my love to her. Love is kind.

Let your gentleness be evident to all. (Phil. 4:5 NIV)

Love does not envy. Like the poem about Holland, love does not look at others and wish that my story looks like their story. There is no longing for something I don't have or discontentment in the heart. My story may not look like your story, but it doesn't mean I'm not content. I have a beautiful story. I have a beautiful life. I have a beautiful daughter. I have a beautiful gift. And I'm blessed. Love does not envy.

Love does not dishonor and has no record of wrong. Going through my divorce, I chose to honor. I did this because I was seeking God, but I also did it for Paige. I kept no record of wrong by choosing to forgive. I did this because this is God's way, but I also did it for me. In doing this, Paige continues to have a great relationship with her dad, and now with her bonus dad. Love honors.

Love protects. I have been Paige's advocate. I have been her voice. I have stood up for things I knew would be best for Paige. I have purposed to protect her heart. Love protects.

Love trusts. There have been many times when Paige's life has been completely out of my control. The only thing I've been able to do is pray and say, "I trust God." I've needed to trust God with Paige's life, knowing He loves her more than I do. She's ultimately His daughter who He put into my care to steward here on the earth. Love trusts.

Love hopes. Love looks beyond the current circumstances and sees more than what is there. I have always had a strong faith. I believe in those things that I do not see.

> Faith is the substance of things hoped for; the evidence of things not seen. (Heb. 11:1 NIV)

Paige's life has given me the opportunity to practice and grow my faith. I've looked at health situations and believed beyond what I've seen in front of me. I have also looked at Paige and been able to see more potential in her than others have. Because of my faith, I'm now in a place where I believe we will see a creative miracle in Paige's body, a healing that no one can deny that God stepped in and did it. This healing will cause many to believe in a God they've never known. Love steps out in faith.

Love perseveres. When faced with adversity, love doesn't give up. I can't imagine my life without Paige, and I can't imagine it looking any other way. No matter how difficult the situations have been, despite the difficulty, giving up was never an option. Paige is such a blessing in my life, as well as in the lives of others. If you were to ask me to do it again, I would, because my life has been more fulfilling by having a child with special needs. I've been blessed by seeing Paige, as well as life, through a different set of lenses. God gave me His perspective of what perfection looks like and what's most important in life. Perseverance is true love.

The Greatest Gift

Paige Has Taught Me

Paige has taught me a different perspective of patience. Although she has her own desires, she's at the mercy of someone else to make those desires happen for her. She's required to wait on other people, their timing, their schedule, and their willingness to make what she would like to happen for her. As she waits, she maintains an even temper, a sense of calmness and peace. She's extremely patient!

Paige has taught me how simple it is to give. She doesn't know the world's value that's been assigned to any object. Therefore her giving doesn't have a dollar amount attached to it. She loves to give people papers, stickers, folders, binders, pens, magazines, and even baggies. To her, these things are as priceless as a rare diamond. Right now, she's giving away homemade bracelets that say "Yay! God." When she gives, it truly comes from her heart. She likes it when people smile and make a big deal about what she's given them. People love receiving gifts from Paige because they know she is thinking about them. She's such a giver!

Paige has taught me that she's brilliant. Paige lives in a world that doesn't cater to her style of communication, yet she desires to communicate and be heard. She's the one required to be creative and think beyond our normal thinking. She comes up with her own language to communicate. When you figure out what she's saying, you realize how creative she was to convey her thought. Who's to say her style of communication is not more "normal" than we think? She also has a keen sense of direction. She's not tall enough to see out of the car windows, but she knows when we are close to significant landmarks. She'll speak up and say we're by so and so, and she's right! She's brilliant!

Paige has taught me how to forgive and move through disappointments quickly while maintaining the same level of joy. When Paige encounters a disappointment, I'll see her processing in her mind what just happened, but then she lets it go. She doesn't dwell on it. Once she moves past something, you'll never see it again. It no longer exists for her. Her demeanor doesn't change throughout this process. Paige is forgiving.

Paige has taught me to be an overcomer because she is one. She's so brave, so strong, so diligent. She's a champion. She's the one who has endured so many surgeries. She's the one who lives with a disability. She didn't choose this life, but she has chosen to live. She's chosen resilience and motivation. But most of all, her heart bubbles up with joy! She's a warrior!

Paige has taught me unconditional love. Through her eyes, everyone's created equal. No matter who you are—even if you're a total stranger—Paige has a way of making everyone feel special. Everyone loves to hear Paige call them by name or for her to come up with a name for them in sign language. When she does this, you know Paige has seen you. She carries such an anointing of the love of Jesus, you feel like that's who you've been with. Paige carries Jesus!

Paige has taught me what various kinds of humor look like. She's funny, and she knows it. She's very animated and has contagious joy! She says things that are off the wall at the most appropriate time, catching everyone off guard. Paige is fun!

Paige has taught me you can find your reflection in just about anything. From a young age, she has loved seeing her reflection in a mirror—it's intriguing to her. She's able to see reflections of herself and others in silverware, on computer and TV screens, on car windows, and in mirrors in unexpected places—you name it, she'll find it. This love of seeing herself and others by means of various objects transitioned to cameras and cell phones. She's become known as a paparazzo, capturing images of herself and others. She's come to know when something is out of the ordinary, and she believes it should be captured forever.

Paige has taught me it's easy to share the gospel. She has no fear of man and approaches people with boldness. She doesn't think twice about what they're going to think—she just knows she wants to pray for them. She's a bold disciple.

Paige has taught me there is always "more"! She doesn't stop. She just wants to go, go, go! Anyone who is around Paige for any length of time will come to know her affectionate love for "more!"

God Has Taught Me

Although I'm a preacher's kid, I didn't know the Bible. I was at church every Sunday, but I remember that as I entered my teens, I had a few conversations about the need for me to go to church. None of my friends went to church, so I didn't see why I needed to go.

I thought going to church was to help people become "good people." I remember sitting at the kitchen table having this discussion with my parents and telling them I believed I was a good person and therefore I didn't need to go to church. I don't remember their answer, but I do know that what I believed didn't change the situation. I continued going to church every Sunday until I was able to make my own decision not to go.

It wasn't until after Paige was born that I realized I needed God. I'd enjoyed my college years, I was in the early years of my career, and life had been just fine without going to church.

What I hadn't realized when Paige was born was that I was a baby Christian. I naturally had a positive attitude, but this wasn't enough—I needed help. It wasn't until I sought answers to relieve me from my own personal pain that God "found" me! He spoke! He spoke to me about "my gift."

This was a good start, but it wasn't enough. I soon discovered that in order for the encouragement from God to stay, it required me to do something. I noticed that God's encouragement can slip away easily. I needed to remind myself continuously of His words to me. I had to keep His words close to my heart and believe His words were true over and over again. I had to speak His words to myself and to others. Doing this helped me to believe.

When the quality of Paige's life was up for discussion, I needed answers again. I consulted books and read articles about children with disabilities or special needs, looking for my answer. But my answer didn't come from the books—it came from God. I heard, "God is going to have the final say over Paige's life," instead of the doctors or me.

Then when Paige came home, I did all the things a new mom would do with their new baby, except I knew there was more. I began to look for this *more* in Paige. I began to see more possibilities than met the eye. I began to ask the question, "How can I make her life better?" What God showed me was that He didn't just give me a gift. He gave me a gift and a blessing! My desire was to steward this blessing well, so I asked God, "What does this look like?"

When Paige almost died in Chicago, I was pressed on all sides. I experienced trauma like I'd never experienced it before in my life. Pain pierced my heart like never before. That's when I found myself in the chapel at the hospital, praying for Paige to live. It was God I sought. I turned to God, asking Him to save her life, and He did.

After Paige survived Chicago, we started taking her to church. For the first time as an adult, I chose to walk through the doors of a church again. This time I went because I could see that the people who go to church are "good people." Drawn to their kindness, I wanted to be around them, and I wanted Paige to be around them.

It wasn't until my divorce that God became more real to me than ever before. One would think the birth of Paige and life up to that point had drawn me close to God, but it didn't. I liked the social aspect of going to church. On the outside, our family had looked like the perfect family. We went to church every Sunday, attended some of the outside functions, and had a lot of friends from church, but my relationship was just that—with the people who went to church, not with God.

During the season of my divorce, I didn't seek people or go to the library this time, I sought God. It was during this season that the Bible became more real to me than ever before. I started understanding Scripture more and more. I began to see that there is more to God than going to church on Sundays.

For the first time in my life, I understood that I could have a relationship with God. I began to understand that He's alive, ready to engage, and more real than I ever thought possible. I came to know that I could go to Him with my questions, and He would answer them because He heard me. In seeking Him, He changed me and increased my faith in Him and also for Paige. I started believing what His Word says about healing, and I now believe it for Paige.

Without a doubt, God is faithful. When we seek Him with all our heart, He will give us the desires of our heart. He brought me a man who loves God like I do. He gave me a man of integrity and who loves Paige. God restored my life and my family through Tommy.

God's purposes are far greater than our purposes. He opens doors no man can shut. He opened a door for Paige to go on her first international mission trip. Her life has more purpose than the doctors or I could ever have known when she was born. She has her own ministry. She carries an anointing that's bigger than she is. She prays for people, and they feel loved, and many are healed.

Dare to Dream

I was once asked to dream and write a script as if it were going to go to a movie producer, believing the story would be used in upcoming interviews, articles, and on the back cover of a DVD. This is what I wrote:

> "Paige has already defied the odds. She is currently a rolling miracle, but will be a walking miracle in the days to come. She lives under an open heaven. She has conversations with angels. She's the opening act of what God is about to do on the earth." —Prophet David Wagner

Paige receives a creative miracle that inspires the multitudes to believe for their miracle. Paige's undeniable miracle brings them into the revelation of a God they didn't know personally, or a God they didn't know at all.

Tommy, Sharon, and Paige are called into a worldwide ministry, telling the world about her story from the uncertainty of life at birth to the manifestation of healing that no one can deny. We all three lay hands on the people we come in contact with. They are healed, set free, and receive salvation! This is my dream. What's yours?

I don't think I'm any different than any other parent. In fact, I don't see that my life with Paige is any different than that of any other parent of a child with special needs. But I've been told my life looks different.

What I've been told is that what others would consider a yoke or a burden is no big deal to me. While others are just barely making it and can barely put one foot in front of the other, I'm "dancing, skipping, leaping, jumping, and walking about."

God is the one who has "chosen me" among many to wear my life well. My desire is to be able to show others how to take the weight off, without removing the responsibility. The responsibility remains, but the burden lifts. It's like the story in the Bible about the men who were given talents. God wanted to see what they would do with what they were given. God wants to see what we will do with what we are given. How are we going to steward the gift He's given to us? We've been chosen.

If you're a parent of a child with special needs or a caregiver in any other capacity, such as caring for a spouse with Alzheimer's or a loved one who's sustained an injury or has an illness that causes your loved one to be different than how you've known them to be, you're the one God has chosen to care for them. You've been chosen out of many.

How deep is your love?

How deep is your love when there are so many unknowns? How deep is your love when things don't go as planned? How deep is your love when it's not easy? How deep is your love when people look at your loved one with curiosity? How deep is your love? Many would say love is the defining characteristic of God's people.

> Greater love has no one than this as to lay one's life down for his friends. (John 15:13)

I am thankful and grateful for the breath in Paige's body, and I stand in awe at how God is using her to further His kingdom. When Paige receives her creative miracle, we know she'll immediately go into full-time ministry. It will be a story of God's glory. Healing will not just come to Paige but to many. Jesus healed all! All means all.

I encourage you to believe. Believe in those things you do not see. Hope for those things God has put into your heart. Love the people God has gifted you with because "every good and perfect gift comes from above."

Faith, hope, love, these three; but the greatest of these is love.
(1 Cor. 13:13)

Life with Paige!

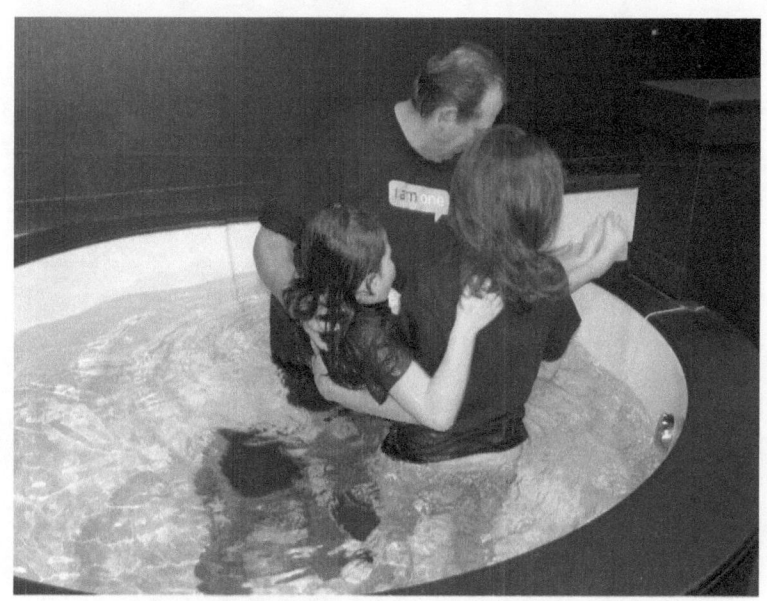

Paige at eighteen years, being baptized

Mother, daughter, God time at the lake

Sharon's dream of Paige's healing captured on canvas—Artist Hannah Aaron

God's restoration—Tommy, Sharon, and Paige

Sharon returns to her place of birth in Guadalajara, Mexico

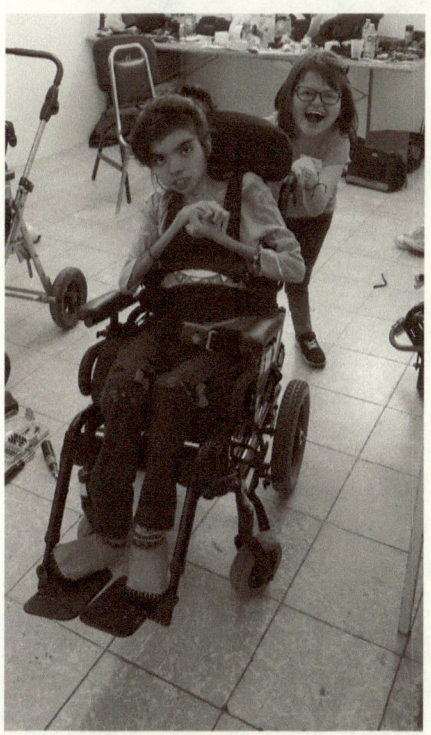

Paige's first mission trip to Guadalajara at age twenty-seven

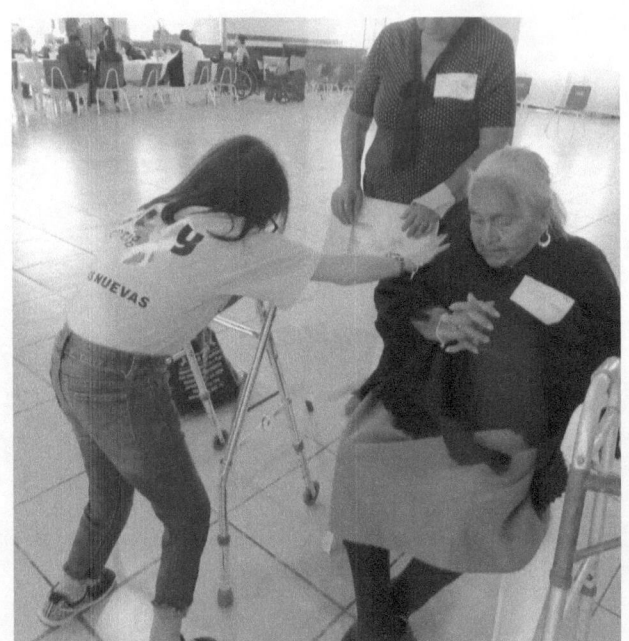

Paige praying in Guadalajara

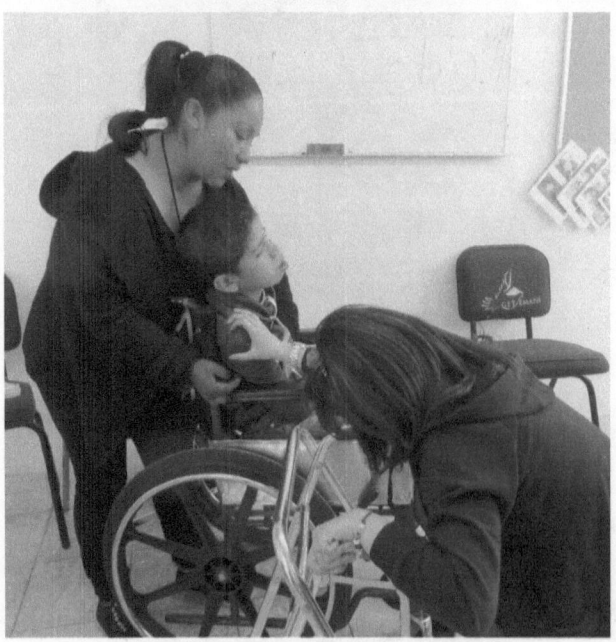

Paige praying in Guadalajara

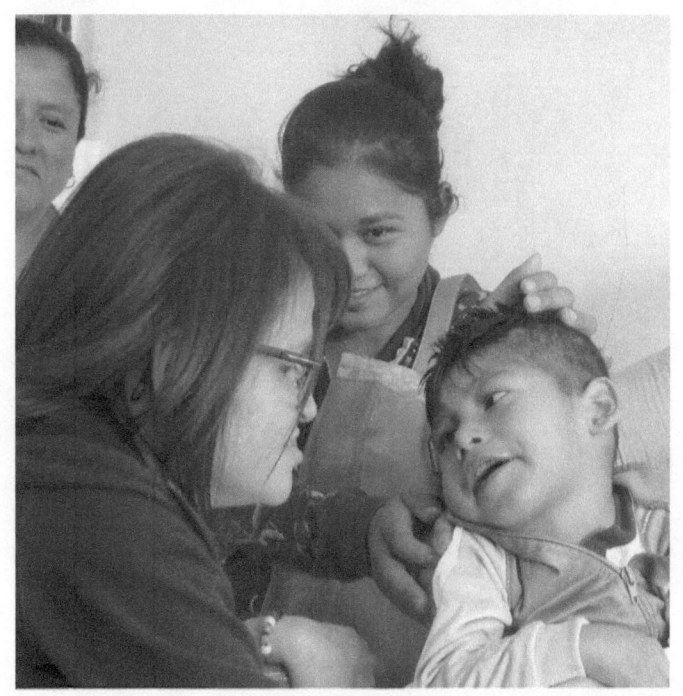

Paige being Paige in Guadalajara

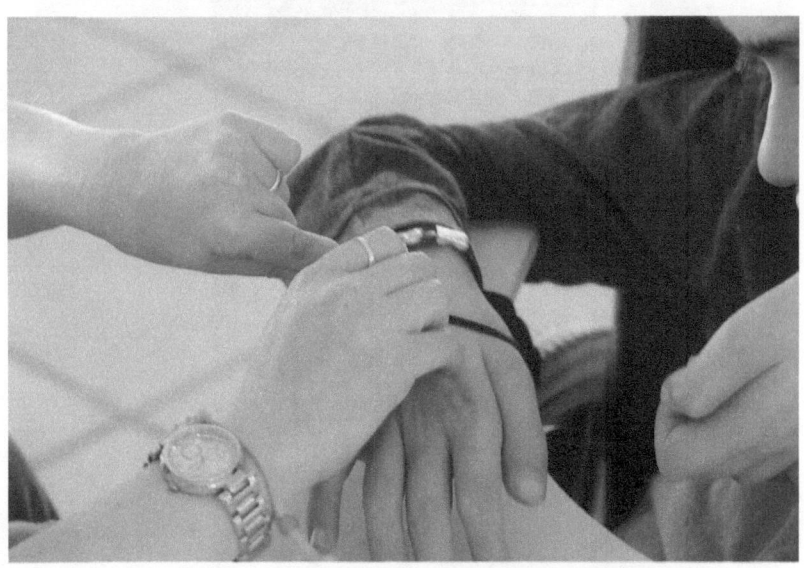

Paige handing out bracelets in Guadalajara

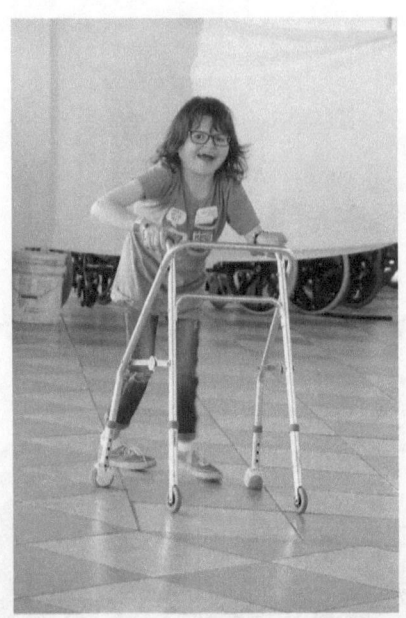

Paige at twenty-eight years old

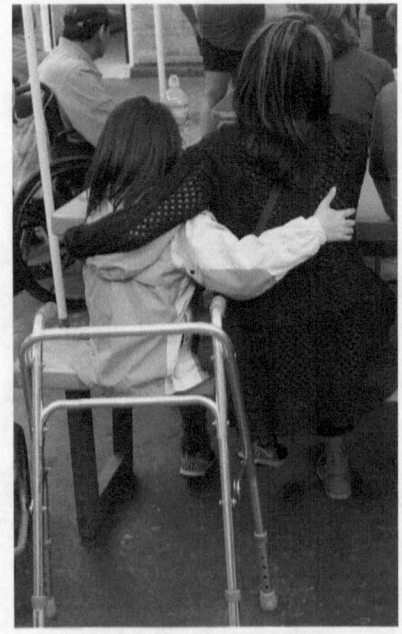

Sharon and Paige—*How Deep Is Your Love?*

The Grandparents

"You are an inspiration to every mother in the world. The way you have taken on the challenges of motherhood with a miracle child is just awesome. Paige is where she is mentally, physically, and emotionally because of you. God knows what He is doing, and He knew the two of you should be together because of the blessing each of you would give the other, and He is up there smiling down on the two of you." **—Cherry/Mother-in-Law**

"I've often said that God knew what He was doing when He gave Paige to you. You, who was so successful in planning for your life as a daughter, a wife, a sister, and a probation officer, quickly accepted Paige's limitations and struggles just to stay alive. There was no, "why me?" feelings apparent in your loving Paige 100 percent while seeking ways to help her progress from the early vegetative state she was in to the current one of a happy communicative Paige who smiles, laughs, verbalizes, and signs, is mobile, and loves school. What a gift you have given her!" **—Joyce/Mother**

"Clearly, God did not have to search far to know who to choose as the best possible mother for Paige! The way you have patiently loved, cared for, and dedicated yourself to transform what could have been a sad story into one of blessing, delight, and joy says it all. What could I possibly add to the commentary of your life? It has been what it means to go the second mile and to love without counting the cost." **—Bob/Daddy**

Yay! God

> I will make them and the places all around My hill a blessing; and I will cause showers to come down in their season; there shall be showers of blessing. (Ezekiel 34:26)

A beautiful exchange of love has taken place in my life, which has resulted in showers of blessings. One of the blessings that continues today are the "Yay! God" bracelets Paige created and gives away.

Paige hands the bracelets out to complete strangers, expecting them to wear it on their wrist. She'll watch until the bracelet is properly in place. Then she smiles with great delight!

God's anointing and light shines on these bracelets. When you receive a bracelet, you've been seen not by Paige but by God. He sees you and He loves you.

Shine bright!

If you would like to have one of the "Yay! God" bracelets, go to our website, http://sharonmrichardson.com. We would like to know who has been blessed by God and Paige through these bracelets. Please email a photo to bracelets@sharonmrichardson.com of you wearing the "Yay! God" bracelet and leave a comment, and we will upload the photo and comment to our website or social media.

Order Information

To order additional copies of this book, please visit
www.sharonmrichardson.com.
Also available on Amazon.com and BarnesandNoble.com

www.ingramcontent.com/pod-product-compliance
Lightning Source LLC
Chambersburg PA
CBHW020528080526
44583CB00013B/779